Nelson English

Developing Non-fiction Skills

3

BOOK THREE

John Jackman   Wendy Wren

OXFORD
UNIVERSITY PRESS

Contents

Unit	DEVELOPMENT Text	SKILLS Word	
1 **Disasters**	The Beaufort Scale	Over-used words – 'nice'	Plurals – words ending with 'o'
2 **Journeys**	The Titanic	Root words, prefixes and suffixes	Prefixes
3 **Space**	Walking on the Moon	Synonyms – levels of meaning	Noun and verb agreement
4 **London**	Getting Around in London	Adverbs	'f' and 'fe' word endings
5 **Flight**	Birds' Wings	Antonyms	Soft and hard 'c'
6 **World Religions**	Religions in the UK	Eponyms	'ou' letter pattern
7 **Night**	The Night Sky	Figures of speech	Pronouns and contractions
8 **Australia**	The Great Barrier Reef	Onomatopoeia	Suffix 'ful'
9 **The Caribbean**	Jamaica	Using a thesaurus	Adding suffixes
10 **Our Planet**	Rainforests in Danger	Using a dictionary	Antonyms
11 **Strange Stories**	The Loch Ness Monster	'ist' letter pattern	Suffixes
12 **Mythical Creatures**	Advertising	Abbreviations and acronyms	'ent' and 'ant' word endings
Check-up			

The Beaufort Scale

When the air moves about we say that the wind is blowing. Sometimes the air moves slowly and we get a gentle breeze. Sometimes it moves very quickly and storms, hurricanes and tornadoes occur.

It is particularly important for sailors to have accurate information about the strength of the wind. In 1806, Sir Francis Beaufort, an Admiral in the British Navy, collected information about the effects of different speeds of the wind at sea and compiled what became known as the Beaufort Scale. It has since been adapted to show the effects of the wind on land and is still in use today.

THE BEAUFORT SCALE

Force	Type of wind	What you can see	Speed
0	calm	smoke rises straight up	below 1 kph (less than 1 mph)
1	light air	smoke shows wind direction	1–5 kph (1–3 mph)
2	light breeze	leaves rustle weather-vanes move	6–11 kph (4–7 mph)
3	gentle breeze	twigs move flags flap	12–19 kph (8–12 mph)
4	moderate breeze	dust and paper are blown around small branches move	20–29 kph (13–18 mph)
5	fresh breeze	small trees sway	30–39 kph (19–24 mph)
6	strong breeze	large branches move umbrellas are difficult to use	40–49 kph (25–31 mph)
7	moderate gale	whole trees bend over it is difficult to stand up	50–61 kph (32–38 mph)
8	fresh gale	twigs break off trees	62–74 kph (39–46 mph)
9	strong gale	chimney pots and roof tiles are blown down	75–88 kph (47–54 mph)
10	storm	trees are uprooted	89–102 kph (55–63 mph)
11	violent storm	general destruction	103–117 kph (64–72 mph)
12	hurricane	coasts are flooded devastation	over 117 kph (73 mph or more)

 Comprehension

A Look at the Beaufort Scale and answer the following questions.
1 What are the effects of a strong breeze?
2 How quickly is the wind travelling during a hurricane?
3 What type of wind is blowing when you can see twigs breaking off trees?
4 What is the force of a wind travelling at 30–39 kph?

B 1 In your own words, explain each word below.
   a accurate   b compiled   c adapted
   d moderate   e destruction   f devastation
2 Why do you think it is important for people to have accurate information about the strength of the wind?

Vocabulary

Over-used words – 'nice'

Sometimes it is better to simply leave out the word 'nice'.

Remember, '**nice**' is a very over-used word and you can usually find a better word to use instead.

A Copy the paragraph below, replacing each 'nice' with another word. You can choose words from the box below, or think of some of your own.

It was a nice day. It was nice to see the sun shining. I put on my nice new trainers. My nice Uncle Clive phoned up and invited us for a nice barbeque. He said he had made some nice kebabs. I was excited about going to Uncle Clive's nice house, seeing my nice cousin Lisa and playing with her nice dog.

| brilliant   sunny   smart   fantastic   new   friendly   kind |
| warm   good   colourful   favourite   fashionable   beautiful |

B 1 Copy each phrase below, replacing 'nice' with a better word.

   a *nice letter*   b *nice holiday*   c *nice jumper*

   2 Use each answer from question 1 in a sentence of your own.

Spelling

Plurals – words ending with 'o'

Many words end with the vowel 'e', but very few end with the other four vowels – 'a', 'i', 'o' and 'u'. Those that do are usually words that have come from foreign languages. For example:
   data   fungi   tornado   Peru   plateau

There are special rules for making **plurals** of words that end with 'o'. Usually, we add 'es'. For example:
   tomato   tomato<u>es</u>   tornado   tornado<u>es</u>

But we simply add 's' for:
- words ending in 'oo'. For example:
  cuckoo   cuckoo<u>s</u>
- 'music' words. For example:
  piano   piano<u>s</u>
- abbreviations (shortened words). For example:
  photo   photo<u>s</u> ('photo' is an abbreviation of 'photograph')

A Write the plural of each word.

1 hero   2 soprano   3 volcano   4 potato

5 disco   6 motto   7 hippo   8 echo

9 cello   10 cockatoo   11 radio   12 banjo

B Use a dictionary or other reference books to find out as much as you can about each word below. For example, where did it first come from, is it short for a longer word, etc.?

1 rhino   2 piano   3 cuckoo   4 photo   5 patio

Grammar

Double negatives

Remember, if there are two negative words in one sentence they can often cancel each other out, and the meaning then becomes positive. This is called a **double negative**. For example:

I <u>couldn't</u> do <u>nothing</u> to stop my umbrella blowing away.

'Couldn't do nothing' means the same as 'could do something'!

A Copy these sentences, filling each gap with 'anything' or 'nothing'.

1 They couldn't see _____ because it was dark.

2 There was _____ I could do about it.

3 They wouldn't do _____ to help me.

4 I can't give you _____ as I haven't any spare cash.

B Make each of these positive sentences into a negative sentence.

1 The rescue services were on the scene quickly.

2 I could hear somebody calling for help.

3 I was very frightened.

Sentence construction

The past tense

There are three ways of making the **past tense** of many verbs:

1 By adding 'd' or 'ed'. For example:

I climb<u>ed</u>

2 By adding 'ing' and putting the auxiliary verb 'was' or 'were' before the main verb. For example:

I <u>was</u> climb<u>ing</u>.   We <u>were</u> climb<u>ing</u>.

3 By adding 'd' or 'ed' and putting the auxiliary verb 'had' before the main verb. For example:

I <u>had</u> climb<u>ed</u>.

A Copy and complete this table.

Verb family name	Past tense – + 'd' or 'ed'	Past tense – 'was'/'were' + 'ing'	Past tense – 'had' + 'd' or 'ed'
to shout	he <u>shouted</u>	he was shouting	he had shouted
to discover	they _____	they _____ _____	they _____ _____
to struggle	she _____	she _____ _____	she _____ _____
to wander	I _____	I _____ _____	I _____ _____
to complain	we _____	we _____ _____	we _____ _____
to hurl	you _____	you _____ _____	you _____ _____

B For each verb, write three past-tense sentences, using each of the three ways of making the past tense. The first one has been done to help you.

1 shelter

They shelter<u>ed</u> from the wind.

He <u>was sheltering</u> from the wind.

I <u>had sheltered</u> from the wind.

2 hurry   3 call   4 rescue   5 escape

Writing

Reports

When you write a **report** you need facts and accurate information. Look at this picture:

26th October, 4 p.m.

The Beaufort Scale contains the information needed to write the following factual report on the strength of the wind at 4 p.m.:

At 4 p.m. on the 26th October, the weather was bright and sunny with a moderate breeze, force 4. The strength of the wind was between 20 and 29 kph (13–18 mph), moving small branches and blowing dust and paper along the street.

The report contains:

the date:	26th October
the time:	4 p.m.
the general weather conditions:	bright and sunny
the strength of the wind:	moderate breeze
the speed of the wind in kph:	20–29
the speed of the wind in mph:	13–18
the force of the wind:	4
the effects of the wind:	small branches moving, paper and dust being blown along the street

A Look at the pictures below. They show the effects of the wind at different times on one day, the 17th May.

7 a.m.

11 a.m.

3 p.m.

7 p.m.

Use what you can see in the pictures and information from the Beaufort Scale on page 4 to write a factual report on the general weather conditions and the wind throughout the day. The report should contain four paragraphs, one for each time of the day.

B You could write about the four pictures on page 10 in a different way for a different audience. Imagine you are writing a letter to a friend or relative describing the 17th May.

What you might put in your letter:

* how you felt about what was happening
* whether you stayed indoors or had to go out
* if you had to change your plans
* the effect of the wind on the things around your home.

What you wouldn't put in your letter:

* the speed of the wind in kph or mph
* the force of the wind.

You would write your letter in a friendly, chatty style which is different from the style of a factual report.

Set out your letter, remembering to include your address and also remembering how to finish a letter to someone you know.

The Titanic

In 1912, the *Titanic* was launched. At the time, it was the largest ship that had ever been built. On the night of 14th April, during its first voyage, the *Titanic* struck an iceberg and sank. More than 1,500 people were killed in the disaster.

Below is part of an account of the sinking of the *Titanic* by Walter Lord, a passenger on the ship who survived the disaster.

As the tilt grew steeper, the forward funnel toppled over. It struck the water on the starboard side with a shower of sparks and a crash heard above the general uproar … The *Titanic* was now absolutely perpendicular. From the third funnel aft, she stuck straight up in the air, her three dripping propellers glistening even in the darkness … Out in the boats, they could hardly believe their eyes. For over two hours they had watched, hoping against hope, as the *Titanic* sank lower and lower. When the water reached her red and green running lights, they knew the end was near … but nobody dreamed it would be like this – the unearthly din, the black hull hanging at ninety degrees, the Christmas-card backdrop of brilliant stars … Two minutes passed, the noise finally stopped, and the *Titanic* settled back slightly at the stern. Then slowly she began sliding under, moving at a steep slant. As she glided down, she seemed to pick up speed. When the sea closed over the flagstaff on her stern, she was moving fast enough to cause a slight gulp.

from *A Night to Remember* by Walter Lord

GLOSSARY
aft towards the back of a ship
flagstaff pole to which a flag is attached
hull the main body of a ship
propellers blades that turn round and move a boat
starboard the right-hand side of a ship
stern the back of a ship

*Walter Lord,
photographed in 1955*

Comprehension

A 1 What do you think caused the 'general uproar' on the ship?

2 What does the writer mean when he says the ship was 'absolutely perpendicular'?

3 What adjective does the writer use to describe the propellers? Why?

4 What were the people in the boats 'hoping against hope' would not happen?

This is an article from the *Daily Herald* of 22nd April, 1912.

Mr C H Stengel, a first-class passenger, said that when the *Titanic* struck the iceberg the impact was terrific, and great blocks of ice were thrown on the deck, killing a number of people. The stern of the vessel rose in the air, and people ran shrieking from their berths below. Women and children, some of the former naturally hysterical, having been rapidly separated from husbands, brothers and fathers, were quickly placed in boats by the sailors, who like their officers, it was stated, were heard by some survivors to threaten men that they would shoot if male passengers attempted to get in the boats ahead of the women. Indeed, it was said that shots were actually heard. Mr Stengel added that a number of men threw themselves into the sea when they saw that there was no chance of their reaching the boats. "How they died," he observed, "I do not know." He dropped overboard, caught hold of the gunwale of a boat, and was pulled in because there were not enough sailors to handle her. In some of the boats women were shrieking for their husbands; others were weeping, but many bravely took a turn at the oars.

GLOSSARY

berths bunks on a ship
gunwale side of a ship
impact effect of a collision

A painting of the Titanic being launched in April 1912 at Southampton.

 Comprehension

B 1 What does the reporter mean when he writes that Mr Stengel was 'a first-class passenger'?
2 Why do you think the women and children were put into the lifeboats first?
3 How do you know that the crew of the *Titanic* tried to stop the male passengers from getting into the lifeboats before the women and children?
4 How does the writer make you feel the panic on the ship?

C Read the two accounts again. There are certain phrases in the newspaper report which show you that the reporter was getting his facts second-hand, for example, 'Mr C H Stengel … said that …'. Can you find any more examples?

Vocabulary

Root words,
prefixes and
suffixes

Remember, a **root word** is a basic word to which **prefixes** and **suffixes**
can be added to make other words from the same word family.

Even *Titanic* has other family words. A dictionary will tell you that the
root word of *Titanic* is 'Titan', a word from Greek, which was the name
of a group of mythical gods called the Titans, who were known for
their great size and strength. Other words in the same family have
similar meanings:

> **titan** a person of very great strength, intelligence or importance
> **titanic** something strong and powerful, like the Titans
> **titanium** a chemical for making very strong metals

A Copy each word below. Underline the root word, and write down
as many words as you can think of from the same word family.
Use a dictionary to help you.

1 *propellers*	2 *surviving*	3 *interviewed*
4 *absolutely*	5 *terrific*	6 *naturally*

B Use a dictionary to check the definition and find the origin of
each word from part A.

Spelling

Prefixes

A Copy the table below and complete it by adding at least three
examples of words using each prefix. Use a dictionary to help you.

Prefix	Meaning	Examples
bi	two	
cent	hundred	
inter	between	
pre	before	
tele	at a distance	
tri	three	
un	not	

B Write some sentences about the *Titanic*, using as many words as
possible that have prefixes from the table in part A.

Grammar

Word order in dialogue

In **dialogue**, words and phrases can often be rearranged and still make sense. The meaning can stay the same, be altered slightly or changec great deal. For example:

"Please help me," the child shouted.

"Please!" the child shouted, "Help me!"

The child shouted, "Please help me."

Each of the three sentences above uses the same words, but in a different order.

You may need to alter the punctuation.

A Re-write each sentence, putting the words or phrases in a different order.

1 "Did you hear that crashing, grinding noise?" said the boy.

2 "No, you settle down and get some sleep," said his mother.

3 "Look, there is water coming under the door!" screamed the boy.

4 "The ship is sinking, and we will all be drowned!" he yelled.

B Copy each sentence below, then write it in two other ways. You may change the orange word in each version if you wish. Tick the version of each sentence that you think makes the strongest statement.

1 "Listen, or we shall all be drowned," called the young officer.

2 "Where is my dear husband?" shouted one woman.

3 "He's a brave man, and I'm sure he'll be safe," said another.

4 "Help, the sea is freezing! Who will help us?" cried an old man.

Sentence construction

Active and passive sentences

Notice how **passive** sentences need a **helper** (auxiliary) **verb**.

Remember, a sentence must have a verb. A sentence is **active** when the person, place or thing that the sentence is about does the action. For example:

The *Titanic* <u>hit</u> the iceberg.

subject	active verb

A sentence is **passive** when the person, place or thing that the sentence is about has the action done to it. For example:

The iceberg <u>was hit</u> by the *Titanic*.

subject	passive verb

A The sentences below are active. Rewrite each sentence, changing it so that it becomes passive. The first one has been done to help you.

1 *The sailor threw a lifebelt.*

   A lifebelt was thrown by the sailor.

2 *The crew helped the women and children.*

3 *People in the lifeboats watched the ship in silence.*

4 *The band played music as the ship went down.*

5 *The newspapers splashed the story all over their front pages.*

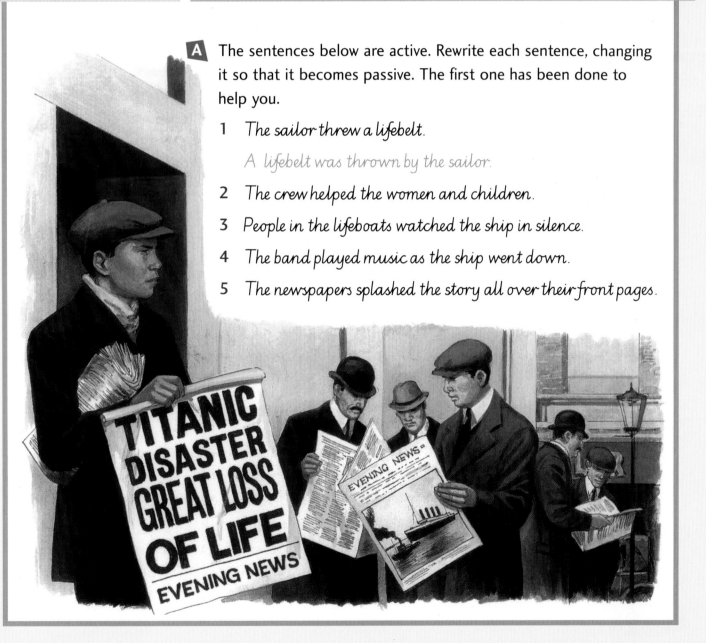

17

B Rewrite each sentence, changing it from passive to active.

1 *The lookout was taken by surprise by the iceberg.*

2 *Children were comforted by their parents.*

3 *Eventually the great ship was swallowed up by the ocean.*

4 *Places in the lifeboats were given up to women and children by some brave men.*

Writing

First- and second-hand accounts

Both the accounts of the sinking of the *Titanic* were written for an **audience** (the people who read them). Their **purpose** was to inform people of the events of that terrible night.

Both Walter Lord and Mr Stengel experienced the disaster. The difference is that:

- Walter Lord recounts his experience himself. We call this a **first-hand account**.
- Mr Stengel's experience is written about by someone else. We call this a **second-hand account**.

A 1 Imagine that you are a survivor of the *Titanic* disaster. Recount what happened to you in a short letter to a friend.

2 Imagine you are a reporter who has interviewed a survivor of the *Titanic* disaster. Write a report about it for your newspaper.

B Read the passage opposite and choose to do one of the following.

- Imagine you are William Reeves and write a letter to a close friend, recounting what happened that night.
- Imagine you are a reporter who has interviewed William Reeves about what happened that night. Write a report about it for your newspaper.

In April 1935, William Reeves, a young sailor, was on watch on the bow of a tramp steamer sailing from Tyneside to Canada. He knew all about April being a bad month for icebergs and he knew that the *Titanic* had been struck at midnight – the hour his watch was to end. He was very worried but was afraid to sound the alarm as his shipmates would make fun of him. He stared ahead into the gloom but could see nothing. Suddenly he remembered the exact date the *Titanic* went down – April 14th 1912 – this was also the day he was born! He shouted a warning and the helmsman stopped the boat only a few yards from an enormous iceberg. The crew soon realised that they were totally surrounded by icebergs and it took a Newfoundland ice-breaker nine days to smash its way through. The name of the tramp steamer was the *Titanian*.

GLOSSARY

helmsman the person who steers a ship
ice-breaker a ship designed to break through ice
tramp steamer a type of ship

Walking on the Moon

Speaking in the early 1960s, the President of the USA, John F Kennedy, said that he wanted the Americans to land a man on the Moon before the end of the decade. In the next few years, many astronauts went up in spacecraft but none actually landed on the Moon. In 1969, the *Apollo 11* spacecraft was launched, with three astronauts aboard.

The first crisis the lunar explorers faced came just short of Moonfall. The *Apollo 11* Lunar Module, code-named *Eagle*, was still 9.5 km (6 miles) up when the vital guidance computer began flashing an alarm – it was overloading. Any second it could give up the ghost under the mounting pressure and nothing the two astronauts could do would save the mission. Emergencies were nothing new to Commander Neil Armstrong but he and his co-pilot, Buzz Aldrin, hadn't even practised for this one on the ground – no one believed it could happen.

Sweeping feet-first towards their target, they pressed ahead as controllers on Earth waited heart-in-mouth. Racing against the computer, *Eagle* slowed and then pitched upright to 'stand' on its rocket plume and give Armstrong his first view of the landing site. The wrong one! They had overshot by four miles into unfamiliar territory and were heading straight for a football-field-size crater filled with boulders 'the size of Volkswagens'.

The Eagle *lunar module above the Moon's surface, with the Earth in the background*

Apollo 11 *about to be launched*

With his fuel running out, and only a minute's flying time left, Armstrong coolly accelerated the hovering *Eagle* beyond the crater, touching 88 kph (55 mph). Controllers were puzzled and alarmed by the unplanned manoeuvres. Mission Director George Hage pleaded silently, 'Get it down, Neil. Get it down.'

The seconds ticked away.

'Forward, drifting right,' Aldrin said. And then, with less than 20 seconds left, came the magic word, 'Contact!'

Armstrong spoke first: 'Tranquility Base here, the *Eagle* has landed.' His words were heard by 600 million people – a fifth of humanity.

About six and a half hours later, *Eagle*'s front door was opened and Armstrong backed out onto a small porch. He wore a £42,000 Moonsuit, a sort of Thermos flask capable of stopping micro-meteoroids travelling 30 times faster than a rifle bullet. He carried a backpack which weighed 49 kg and had enough oxygen for four hours. Heading down the ladder, Armstrong unveiled a £200,000 TV camera so the world could witness his first step: 'That's one small step for a man, one giant leap for mankind.' It was 3.56 a.m. on 20th July, 1969.

GLOSSARY
crater a large hollow in the ground
lunar of the Moon
micro-meteoroids small objects that travel through space

Buzz Aldrin walking on the Moon (photographed by Neil Armstrong)

Comprehension

A
1. What was the code name for the Lunar Module?
2. Who was Armstrong's co-pilot?
3. What was the name of the site where the Lunar Module landed?
4. How much did Armstrong's backpack weigh?
5. What was the time and date of Armstrong's first steps on the Moon?

B
1. Why do you think the astronauts needed a 'guidance computer'?
2. What does the author mean when he writes:
   a. 'They had overshot by four miles'?
   b. 'Armstrong coolly accelerated the hovering *Eagle*'?
3. Why is Armstrong's moonsuit described as 'a sort of Thermos flask'.
4. Where do you think the third astronaut was when the Lunar Module landed on the Moon?

C These are notes the writer might have made about the Moon landing. Write them in the correct order.

they were 6.33 km (4 miles) from where they planned to land

they had very little fuel left

the guidance computer was not working properly

they had only 20 seconds to land

they were heading for a crater with enormous boulders

they made a soft Moon landing and were the first humans to land on the Moon

Vocabulary

Synonyms – levels of meaning

Remember, **synonyms** are words or phrases that have similar meanings. However, there are usually slight differences in meaning between synonyms. You need to select the word that has the most accurate meaning for whatever you are writing.

A Write as many synonyms as you can think of for each word in green.

1 The first *crisis* the lunar explorers faced …

2 … the *vital* guidance computer

3 … it would *give up the ghost* …

4 … under the *mounting* pressure …

5 *Heading* down the ladder …

We can usually rank a set of synonyms in order, from 'least' to 'most'. For example, these words are synonyms that show varying levels of pleasure, from 'pleased' to 'ecstatic':

pleased   excited   thrilled   delighted   overjoyed   ecstatic

B Use a thesaurus to find as many synonyms as possible for each word below. Then, write out the synonyms for each word in order, from 'least' to 'most'.

1 a *big*   b *silly*   c *kind*   d *fast*

2 Write a sentence using the 'most' word in each set of words from question 1.

Spelling

Noun and verb agreement

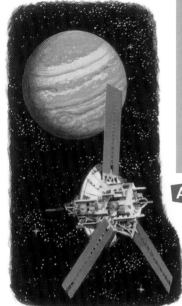

Remember, to make a **noun plural** we normally add 's'. For example:

| star | star<u>s</u> |
| astronaut | astronaut<u>s</u> |

But, if the noun ends with 's', 'x', 'ch' or 'sh', we add 'es'. For example:

| bu<u>s</u> | bus<u>es</u> |
| chur<u>ch</u> | church<u>es</u> |

If a noun ends in 'y', we change the 'y' to 'i' and add 'es'. For example:

| stor<u>y</u> | stor<u>ies</u> |

But, if the letter before the 'y' is a vowel, we simply add 's'. For example:

| da<u>y</u> | day<u>s</u> |

A Write the plural of each noun.

1 satellite	2 camera	3 activity	4 alley
5 planet	6 difficulty	7 valley	8 quay
9 company	10 boulder	11 torch	12 ceremony

Remember, the rules are the same for adding 's' and 'es' to **verbs**.
However, we usually add 's' or 'es' to a verb when it goes with a <u>singular</u> noun! For example:

| the spaceships crash | the spaceship crash<u>es</u> |
| the astronauts escape | the astronaut escap<u>es</u> |

B Write each verb as it would be used with a <u>singular</u> noun.

1 lift	2 crash	3 push	4 lurch
5 try	6 play	7 shout	8 climb
9 bend	10 crouch	11 fly	12 wash

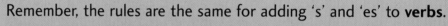

Grammar

Direct and reported speech

Speech marks are also called inverted commas.

Direct speech is when you write the actual words that a person has spoken. We show this by putting **speech marks** (" ") around the spoken words. For example:

"Contact!" said Buzz Aldrin.

Reported speech or **indirect speech** is when you write about (or report) what a person has said, without using the actual words spoken, so you don't need speech marks. For example:

Buzz Aldrin said that they had contact.

A Write each of these sentences as reported speech.

1 "The guidance computer is flashing," said the engineer.
2 "We can't possibly land in this crater!" exclaimed Buzz Aldrin.
3 "No," agreed Armstrong. "We'll keep going for a while."
4 "You had me worried," admitted the Controller.

B Write each of these sentences as direct speech.

1 Armstrong asked Aldrin to check their position.
2 Buzz Aldrin reported that they had landed safely.
3 Mission Control told the astronauts it was time to return to Apollo 11.
4 The President told the astronauts that he and all the American people were proud of their achievement.

Sentence construction

Active and passive sentences

Remember, a sentence is **active** when the person, place or thing that the sentence is about does the action. For example:

The astronauts <u>collected</u> their equipment.

subject   active verb

A sentence is **passive** when the person, place or thing that the sentence is about has the action done to it. For example:

The equipment was <u>collected</u> by the astronauts.

subject   passive verb

A Rewrite these sentences, changing them from active to passive. The first one has been done to help you.

1 The Sun lights the Earth.

The Earth is lit by the Sun.

2 Huge meteorites hit Jupiter in 1994.

3 The scientists photographed the eclipse of the Sun.

4 Millions of people watched the Apollo 11 mission on television.

5 Neil Armstrong opened the door of the module.

B Rewrite these sentences, changing them from passive to active.

1 Buzz Aldrin was amazed by the beauty of the Earth.

2 The girls were fascinated by the vastness of the universe.

3 The Moon was eclipsed by the Sun.

4 Rock samples were collected by the astronauts.

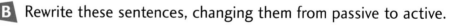

Writing

Reports

When you write a **report** about something that has happened, you need to make it as easy as possible for the reader to follow the events.

- Your first paragraph should say what you are going to write about.
- Present the events in the order in which they happened.
- The style should be formal, not chatty, as it would be in conversation or in a letter to a friend. For example, 'Emergencies were nothing new', not 'Loads of things went wrong'; 'Controllers were puzzled and alarmed', not 'The bosses were in a flap'.
- Use words and phrases to show the passing of time. For example, 'the seconds ticked away' or 'About six and a half hours later'.

Imagine you were with Neil Armstrong on the day he landed on the Moon. Mission Control has asked you to write a report about the things that happened from the moment you set foot on the Moon to when you returned to the Lunar Module.

A Think about your first paragraph. Explain who you are and what you were doing. Include these important names and dates:

Buzz Aldrin	Neil Armstrong	20th July, 1969
your name	The Eagle	Apollo 11	Tranquility Base

Make notes on the events which might have taken place, such as:

walking on the Moon	collecting rock samples
speaking to Mission Control	anything unusual or exciting
planting the flag	returning to *Eagle*

Number your notes in the order you think they happened.

B Write your report. Remember:
- Your first paragraph should make it clear to the reader what the report is about.
- Write about the events in the order in which they happened.
- Use a new paragraph for each event.
- Think about the purpose of the report and the audience – who you are writing for. Do not write as if you were sending a chatty letter to a friend.

Getting around in London

The Underground

The London Underground (or Tube) runs for twenty hours a day, serving all parts of central London. Maps on leaflets and in Underground stations show every Tube line by name and in a different colour. This makes it simpler to plan your route to all the city's main attractions, most of which are close to stations.

The Tube is divided into six fare zones. Zone 1 covers central London. Please make sure your ticket covers all the zones you will be travelling through. If it doesn't, you will be liable to a penalty fare.

Many Underground stations now have automatic ticket gates. Simply insert your ticket face up then retrieve it to open the gate. At the end of your journey, if the value of travel on your ticket is used up, the gate will open but your ticket will be retained.

Buses

With 17,000 bus stops all over London you're never far from a bus route. The bus network is divided into four fare zones. Bus Zone 4 covers approximately the same area for bus travel only as Zones 4, 5 and 6 do for the Underground and National Railways. You either show your Travelcard or Bus Pass or pay the driver or conductor. Please ensure you have the right ticket for your journey. If it isn't valid you will be liable to a penalty fare.

There are two types of bus stop:

 compulsory, where buses always stop unless full

 request, where you stop a bus by putting out your hand.
If already full, however, the bus may not stop. To get off at a request stop, ring the bell once in good time to let the driver know. N-prefixed Night Buses treat all stops as request stops.

Many London buses are red, though some appear in other colours. All buses operating on a London Transport bus route will display this sign.

London Transport Bus Service

Night time travel

Daytime buses and the Underground run until approximately 12.30 p.m. But our extensive system of Night Buses operates throughout the night. Nearly all Night Buses pass through Trafalgar Square, serving central London's many bars, clubs, restaurants, theatres and cinemas.

Night Bus fares are slightly higher than in the daytime, and child fares are not available. All Night Bus route numbers start with the letter 'N'.

One Day tickets, including Family or Visitor Travelcards, cannot be used on N-prefixed Night Buses. One Day and Two Day Visitor Travelcards are also not accepted.

Staying safe

General advice

- Smoking is not permitted on the Underground or on buses.
- Please keep personal belongings with you at all times to avoid delays caused by security alerts. (Abandoned luggage may be destroyed.)
- Be aware that pickpockets operate in busy areas.
- Please take note of all safety notices and, in the unlikely event of an emergency, follow the instructions of our trained staff.
- Travelling is easier and more comfortable outside of the busy 'rush hour': 8 a.m. – 9.30 a.m. and 5 p.m. – 6 p.m. Mondays to Fridays.

Lifts and escalators

- Keep loose clothing and luggage clear of lift doors.
- On escalators take extra care with children.
- Pushchairs and buggies should be folded.
- Be careful when stepping on or off an escalator, especially when carrying luggage.

Platforms

- Do not stand near the edge.
- NEVER try to pick up any belongings that have fallen onto the track, as it is electrified. Staff will assist you.

Trains and buses

- NEVER obstruct doors or try to get on or off as the doors are closing.
- Mind the gap between the train and platform edge when entering or leaving a train.
- Only get on or off a bus when it is stationary at a bus stop.

Comprehension

A 1 Find and copy a short piece of information from the leaflet about travelling on:
   a the Underground
   b London buses

2 Find and copy an instruction from the leaflet about travelling on:
   a the Underground
   b London buses

B 1 Find and copy an instruction that tells you what you must do in order to stay safe when travelling on buses and Tube trains.

2 Find and copy an instruction that tells you what you must <u>not</u> do in order to stay safe when travelling on buses and Tube trains.

C Choose three instructions given in the leaflet, and explain why you think travellers should take notice of them.

Vocabulary

Adverbs

Remember, **adverbs** can tell us how words are spoken. They add detail and variety to your writing. For example:

"Hurry up," snapped the boy, <u>rudely</u>.

Remember, most **adverbs** end with 'ly'. You may need to change the word slightly when you add the suffix.

A Make an adverb from each word.

1	quick	2	cross	3	sharp
4	aggression	5	kind	6	positive
7	polite	8	abrupt	9	happiness
10	anger	11	stupid	12	slow
13	cheerful	14	sad	15	grumpiness

B 1 Copy this piece of dialogue, filling each gap with an adverb.

"Could you help me?" the tourist said _____ .

"Do you want to buy a paper?" asked the paper seller _____ .

"No, I need to get to St Paul's Cathedral," said the tourist _____ .

"There's hundreds of ways to get there," snapped the newspaper seller _____ .

"I only need one," responded the tourist _____ .

"And I only need to sell papers!" retorted the newspaper seller _____ .

2 To continue the argument in question 1, write two more things each person said. Use an adverb in each piece of dialogue.

Spelling

'f' and 'fe' word endings

Remember, most spelling rules have some exceptions!

Remember, it can be tricky to make the plural forms of nouns that end with '**f**' or '**fe**'. We usually change the 'f' or 'fe' to 'v' and add 'es'.
For example:

wolf   wol<u>ves</u>   wife   wi<u>ves</u>

When a word ends with 'ff', we just add 's'. For example:

cuff   cuff<u>s</u>

A Write the answer to each clue. The answers are all plurals.
The singular form of each answer ends in 'f' or 'fe'.

1 _____ fall off the trees in autumn.
2 _____ are used with forks.
3 Bread dough is formed into _____ .
4 Tribal leaders are often called _____ .
5 People who steal are called _____ .
6 _____ keep our necks warm.
7 Young cattle are called _____ .
8 We blow our noses on _____ .
9 A whole is made up of two _____ .
10 Large, wild dogs are called _____ .

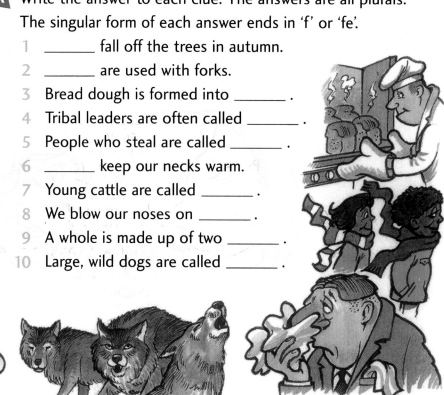

A few 'f'/'fe' words are both nouns and verbs. The nouns are made plural by adding 's', but have a 'ves' ending when they are verbs.

B 1 Write a sentence using each pair of words below, to show that you know what they mean.

a *safe   saves*   b *belief   believes*

2 Write a short story about a family of elves, using as many plural words ending in 'ves' as you can.

Grammar

Noun and verb agreement

Remember, the **noun(s)** and **verb(s)** in a sentence have to **'agree'**. The verb you should use depends on whether the noun is singular or plural. Use 'is' and 'was' with a singular noun. For example:

Past tense: The tourist <u>was</u> on the tube train.

> singular noun

Present tense: The tourist <u>is</u> on a bus.

> singular noun

Use 'are' and 'were' with a plural noun, or with 'you', whether it is singular or plural. For example:

Past tense: The tourists <u>were</u> on the tube train.

> plural noun

Present tense: Now the tourists <u>are</u> on a bus.

> plural noun

Past tense: "You <u>were</u> on the train, too, weren't you, Jane?"

> singular

Present tense: "You <u>are</u> kind to wait for me," I said to the girls.

> plural

A Copy and complete these past-tense sentences.

1 We __were__ planning to visit Buckingham Palace.

2 I __was__ really looking forward to it.

3 Simon __was__ hoping to see the Changing of the Guard.

4 We could hardly see because there __were__ so many people.

5 The crowd __was__ huge.

6 I asked if we __were__ standing in the right place.

B Copy and complete these present-tense sentences.

1 "Buckingham Palace __is__ always busy at this time," explains the policeman.

2 " __Is__ the crowd always this big?" asks Dad.

3 "Usually, there __are__ fewer people in the afternoons," replies the policeman.

4 "Thanks, that __is__ very helpful," says Dad.

Sentence construction

Imperative verbs

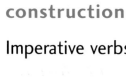

Commands often end with an exclamation mark.

The **imperative** form of a verb comes from the verb family name.
Imperatives are mainly used in instructions and commands. For example:

Verb family names:

to break   to beat   to stop   to come

Instructions: <u>Break</u> three eggs into a bowl. <u>Beat</u> them with a fork.

Commands: <u>Stop</u> that! <u>Come</u> here immediately!

Imperatives are also used in invitations, advice and pleas. For example:

Invitations: Do <u>come</u> to my party.
Advice: <u>Stop</u> eating junk food.
Plea: Please <u>forgive</u> me!

A Use the verb family names in the box to help you complete the commands below.

| to roll | to peel | to go | to plant | to tidy | to eat |

1 <u>To peel</u> four apples.
2 <u>To eat</u> your dinner while it is hot.
3 <u>To go</u> up to your bedroom!
4 <u>To tidy</u> up this classroom!
5 <u>To roll</u> the dice.
6 <u>To plant</u> the seeds about 2 cm apart.

B 1 Use the imperative to write three commands.
2 Use the imperative to write three instructions.

Eat your dinner!   Spread the honey then butter.
Brush your teeth!
Go to bed!

Writing

Instructions

Instructions and **rules** are similar. They tell us what to do and what not to do. They are written for various reasons. For example:

- how to make something
- how to do something
- how to stay safe.
- how to play a game
- how to get somewhere

Instructions can be quite long and detailed. They may be numbered and often have to be read and followed in a set order. Rules are usually quite short and simple and often tell us what to do and what not to do. A set of rules can usually be read and understood in any order.

Troll   Mabbit

Look at the map of the Dark Lands below. Mabbit and Troll have to get from the Marshlands to the mountain where the treasure is hidden. Imagine you have been on this journey and know the best way to go. Write some <u>instructions</u> for Mabbit and Troll. Make up some instructions about what they will need to take with them (for example, a rope) and what they need to collect on the way (for example, a key).

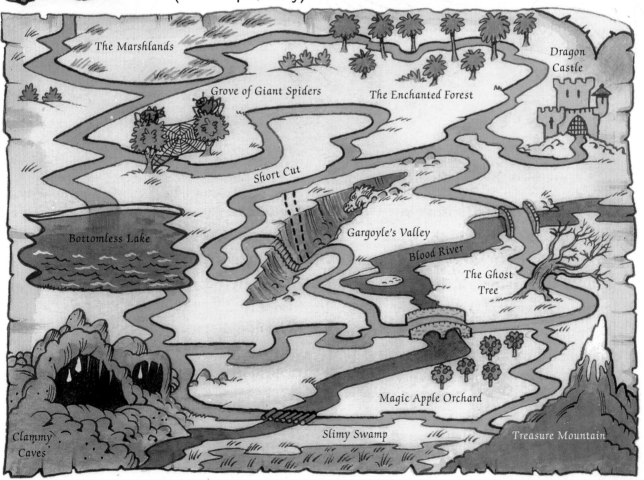

A bird's wing is a very complicated 'arm', made up of bones covered with a layer of feathers. The basic structure of all birds' wings is the same, but the shape and size varies, depending on the way each type of bird lives, feeds and flies. The wings need to be strong enough to support the bird's weight in flight. The feathers have to be 'self-smoothing', tough enough to cope with knocks and bumps, and renewable, so that if one is lost it can be replaced.

How Birds Fly

Donald Buzzard

enlargement of feather structure

bone structure of wing

feathers

The bodies of birds have evolved over thousands of years to be of minimum weight. 'They have a skull that is the lightest of all creatures, their bones are hollow yet strong, and they have no teeth or heavy jaws.'[1] However, they have a large, immensely strong heart and very powerful breast muscles that account for half their total body weight.

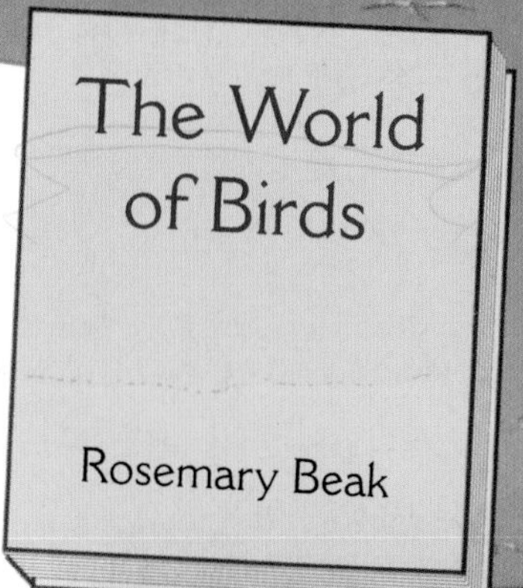

[1] *The Anatomy of Birds* by J. Wing

so they can carry their own body weight.

The World of Birds

Rosemary Beak

Birds' wings can be many shapes and sizes. As Donald Buzzard tells us in his book *How Birds Fly*, the shape and size of each type of bird's wings suit the way that bird flies. Some birds fly quite slowly, whereas others have to fly very quickly, like the peregrine falcon, which can reach speeds of nearly 300 km an hour as it pursues its prey (about the speed of the world's fastest express train).

A Bird Watcher's Guide

Sam Twitcher

Long wings are best for gliding. Most gulls have long, narrow wings and can glide for hundreds of kilometres. This albatross glides so well, it can even sleep while flying!

albatraz prison.

Short wings allow a bird to twist and turn quickly. Woodland and garden birds, like sparrows, starlings and this kingfisher, have short wings, because they need to rapidly change direction as they fly among the branches of trees.

Broad, large wings are best for soaring high above the ground. This eagle, like many other birds of prey, makes use of thermals (currents of warm air) to lift it high in the sky, as it scans the ground below for prey.

Comprehension

A

1 Which book provides information about the structure of birds' bodies?

2 Which book provides information about different types of birds' wings?

3 Which book provides information about feathers?

B Use a dictionary to find the meanings of the following words.

1 evolved	2 minimum	3 gliding
4 soaring	5 hover	6 anatomy

C Carefully re-read the extract from *A Bird Watcher's Guide* on page 37. Make notes on the information by copying key words and phrases.

Vocabulary

Antonyms

Remember, **antonyms** are words that mean the opposite. For example:

fast   slow   maximum   minimum   broad   narrow

A Write an antonym for each of these words.

1 high	2 loose	3 straight	4 up
5 wide	6 efficient	7 cover	8 disapprove

Some words do not have an antonym. For example:

bird   glide

B 1 Write the headings 'Has an antonym' and 'Doesn't have an antonym'. Write each word from the box under the correct heading, and write at least one antonym for each word that has one.

> many   wing   copy   long   most   sleep   and
> branches   top   eagle   high   hover   down
> rough   feather   sure   strong   fall

2 Look at the lists you wrote in question 1. Write some sentences about what you notice.

Hint: What types of words can have opposites? Why can some words have more than one antonym?

Spelling

Soft and hard 'c'

A 1 Sort these words into lists, depending on the letter that follows the 'c'.

> cap December cinema certain cabin celery centre
> pencil cigar city casualty ferocity excellent
> cotton citizen process incapable cement decide
> cat century camel acid car

2 What do you notice about how the sound the 'c' makes is affected by the letter that follows it?

When a 'c' makes an 's' sound, it is called a **soft 'c'**. For example:
   rice   cinema

When a 'c' makes a 'k' sound, it is called a **hard 'c'**. For example:
   comb   candle

B 1 Make a list of all the hard 'c's in this limerick, and a list of all the soft 'c's.
There was an old man, Vince Price,
Who thought that birds were nice
Until, with a glance,
He saw, quite by chance,
They were eating his curry and rice!

2 Write a limerick of your own, using as many hard and soft 'c's as possible. You may find some of the rhyming words from this table helpful.

dance	fence	ice	prince	ace	ounce
glance	pence	rice	mince	race	bounce
prance	commence	price	wince	face	pounce
chance	consequence	slice	since	lace	flounce

Grammar

Abstract nouns

An **abstract noun** is the name of an idea, feeling or quality that you can't touch, taste, smell, hear or see. For example:

Qualities: bravery   enthusiasm   weakness
Feelings: sadness   worry   anger

A Sort these nouns into two lists – common nouns and abstract nouns.

strength   wings   determination   feather   hope   sadness
delight   girl   clouds   sorrow   joyfulness   sky

Abstract nouns can be made from common nouns, adjectives and verbs.

B 1 Make an abstract noun from each of these common nouns. The first one has been done to help you.

a friend   *friendship*
b knight   c thief   d sick
e leader   f brother   g hero

2 Make an abstract noun from each of these adjectives. The first one has been done to help you.

a dark   *darkness*
b moist   c grateful   d empty
e weary   f horrible   g cruel

3 Make an abstract noun from each of these verbs. The first one has been done to help you.

a to observe   *observation*
b to create   c to punish   d to encourage
e to hate   f to grieve   g to please

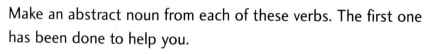

Sentence construction

Compound sentences

Short sentences can be joined together by **conjunctions** to make **compound sentences**. For example:

The kingfisher has short wings. It flies very fast.

The kingfisher has short wings <u>and</u> it flies very fast.

conjunction

A Join each pair of sentences with the conjunction 'and' or 'but'.

1 Humans can fly. They need machines to help them.

2 The bird flies fast. It catches the moth.

3 The kestrel swoops down on its prey. The mouse escapes.

4 Concorde can fly quickly. Kestrels can hover or fly quickly.

5 I enjoy bird-watching. I often sketch the birds I see.

B Copy each sentence, choosing 'until', 'so', 'because' or 'but' to complete it.

1 I hid behind the hedge _____ I could watch the birds.

2 The gull glided along the cliff _____ it reached its nesting place.

3 The eagle has sharp claws _____ it can grasp its prey.

4 Short wings are good for twisting and turning _____ long wings are better for gliding.

5 Birds of prey have broad, large wings _____ they need to be able to soar high in the sky.

Writing

Sources

A **source** is where we get our information from. It might be a book, a magazine, a CD-ROM or a website. When you write information text, it is very important to acknowledge your sources – to say where you got your information from. This can be done in several different ways.

- When you are researching a subject, keep a list of the books and magazines you have used. At the end of your final draft, put in a list of the sources, with the writers' names in alphabetical order. This list is called a **bibliography**. For example:

Bennet, Simon *Capital Cities*
Franks, L. *The City of London*
West, Pauline *Paris, A City Tour*

- Sometimes you may want to use the exact words somebody else has written. This is called **quoting**. You should put the words in quotation marks to show that somebody else wrote or said them. Quotes are often numbered and, at the bottom of the page on which a quote appears, the number is written, with details of where the quote came from. This is called a **footnote**. There is an example of a footnote in the extract from *The World of Birds* by Rosemary Beak, on page 36.

powerful breast muscles that account for half their total body weight.

[1] *The Anatomy of Birds* by J. Wing

- Sometimes, you may want to give the reader an idea of what somebody else has said or written, but you don't have to use their exact words. You can do this by putting their opinion or fact in your own words, then mentioning the name of the writer and the book that the information came from. This is what Sam Twitcher has done, in the extract from his book on page 37. He has mentioned something that Donald Buzzard says in his book.

sizes. As Donald Buzzard tells us in his book *How Birds Fly*, the shape and size of each type of bird's wings suit the way that bird flies. Some birds fly quite slowly,

A 1 Imagine that the information from the three passages on pages 36 and 37 has been used to write a report about birds. Use the authors' names and the titles of their books to write a bibliography for the report.

2 Here are some books that have been used to write a report on fishing. Write a bibliography to go with the report.

B Choose an animal or group of animals to research. Here are some suggestions:

- bee
- tiger
- kangaroo
- tortoise

1 Begin by writing notes on what you already know about the animal. Use your class and school library and a computer to find out more information. Remember, make notes, don't copy out lots of sentences, and keep a list of the books you use.

2 Use your notes to write a short report. Include a quote from one of the books you have used. Number the quote and write the source of the quote at the bottom of the page.

3 Acknowledge your sources by writing a bibliography to go at the end of your report.

Religions in the UK

Religion is one way in which human beings attempt to understand the meaning of life. Many religions are based on following the teachings of a god or gods. The major religious groups are all hundreds of years old, but other religions were founded more recently. There are many different religions all over the world and it is impossible to be certain how many religions there are in Britain, or how many people in Britain belong to each religious group. However, we can be reasonably sure that the main religions in Britain are:

- Judaism

- Islam

- Christianity

- Hinduism

- Sikhism

Other religions practised in Britain include Buddhism, Jainism, Rastafariansim, Shintoism, the Baha'i faith and Zoroastrianism.

Around the world, the calendars of dates and seasons can vary. Many calendars are based on dates that are important in a religion, such as the date when a major religious figure was born. In Britain, we use a calendar that dates from when Jesus Christ was born. The years have been divided up into those before the birth of Christ (BC) and those after the birth of Christ (AD). The table below shows when the major religions had their beginnings, based on the dates of the Christian calendar.

about 2000 BC	early Judaism was founded. Judaism had no single founder, but Abraham lived about 1750 BC
about 1500 BC	early Hinduism was founded. Hinduism had no single founder
about 600 BC	the birth of Zoroaster, the founder of Zoroastrianism
about 599 BC	the birth of Mahavira, the founder of Jainism
about 528 BC	the foundation of Buddhism, founded by Buddha, who lived at around this time
0	the birth of Jesus Christ, the founder of Christianity
about AD 570	the birth of Mohammed, the 'messenger' of Islam
AD 1469	the birth of Guru Nanak, the founder of Sikhism
AD 1817	the birth of Baha'ullah, the founder of the Baha'i faith

While the main religions in the UK have different traditions and ways of worship, many believe that there is only one God for all people and share these four principles, which they believe to be important:
- helping poorer countries
- protecting the environment
- encouraging people of different racial groups to live together peacefully
- promoting world peace.

People who cannot decide whether there is a God call themselves **agnostic**. The word 'agnostic' comes from the Greek for 'not knowing'. Many people have no religious belief, but most believe they have responsibilities to their fellow human beings and to the planet which we all share. Some of these people call themselves **humanists**. **Atheists** are people who are certain that there is no God.

Comprehension

A Copy and complete these sentences.

1 *The five major religious groups in Britain are* _____.

2 *Humanists have no specific religious beliefs but believe* _____.

3 *Agnostics are* _____.

4 *Those who are sure that there is no God are called* _____.

5 *Jesus Christ was born* _____ *Buddha.*

B 1 Explain the following words and phrases in your own words.
    a were founded
    b different traditions
    c principles
    d promoting world peace

2 Look at the information in the box on page 45. Would this have been better presented as a paragraph of text? Give reasons for your answer.

3 Which do you think is the most important of the 'four principles' that the main religions agree about? Give reasons for your answer.

C 1 How many paragraphs are there in the information about religions on pages 44–45?

2 Write brief notes saying what each paragraph is about.

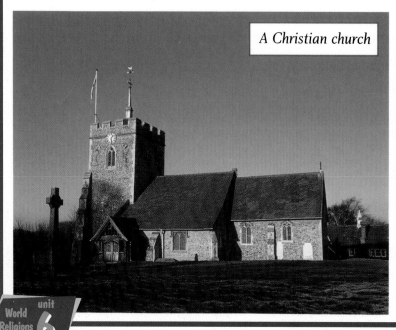

A Christian church

A Muslim mosque

Vocabulary

Eponyms

Several of the names of religions are **eponyms**. An eponym is a word or title that is based on a person's name. For example:

<u>Buddhism</u> is named after Buddha.

<u>Wellingtons</u> or <u>wellington boots</u> are named after the Duke of Wellington.

A Write down the names of two other religious groups that are eponyms.

B Choose five eponyms from the box and research them, using dictionaries, an encyclopaedia and any other suitable reference books. Find the definition of each word and discover all you can about its origin.

guillotine Pennsylvania volt pasteurise saxophone mackintosh cardigan sandwich biro quisling shrapnel Braille

Spelling

'ou' letter pattern

Some letter patterns have more than one sound. The '**ou**' letter pattern can make four different sounds. For example:

Many religi<u>ou</u>s gr<u>ou</u>ps w<u>ou</u>ld be f<u>ou</u>nded in Britain.

A 1 Sort the words from the box into four lists, according to the different sound the 'ou' makes in each word.

soup out group should nervous enormous would famous south dangerous found various sounds could pouch

2 Make up a sentence that contains at least one word from each list you made in question 1.

B

1   Write three words that rhyme with each of the following words.

   a   trout   b   hound   c   slouch

2   Write down which adjective from the adjective box is from the same word family as each noun from the noun box.

Nouns
fame   nerve   danger
glamour   number   victory
suspicion   caution

Adjectives
victorious   numerous   glamorous
nervous   cautious   famous
dangerous   suspicious

Grammar

Collective nouns

Some **proper nouns** are also **abstract nouns**, because we cannot see, touch or smell them. For example: Buddhism, January, Passover.

Remember, **common nouns** are the names of ordinary places and things. For example:

   synagogue   book

Proper nouns are the names of people, countries, special days, etc. For example:

   Christmas   Mohammed

Abstract nouns are the names of ideas and feelings that you can't see, touch or smell. For example:

   sadness   belief

Collective nouns are the names of groups or collections of things or people. For example:

   congregation   crowd

A   Which collective noun would you use for each of the following groups?

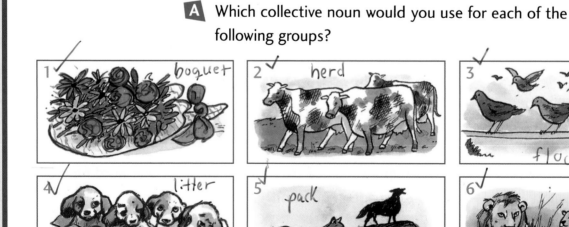

1 boquet   2 ✓ herd   3 ✓ flock

4 ✓ litter puppies   5 ✓ pack   6 ✓ pride

B ✓1 Write down the four words from the box that are common nouns.

book happiness table religious church
candle Buddha flock Sikhism

2 ✓ Write down the four words from the box that are proper nouns.

music excitement Diwali religion band
Jesus Jewish sadness Muslim

3 Write down the four words from the box that are abstract nouns.

choir religion London driver danger
love victory crew person

4 Write down the four words from the box that are collective nouns.

audience anger troop sword car
teacher bunch Hinduism shoal

Sentence construction

Avoiding repetition

Remember, it is important to carefully choose the right words to make your writing more interesting. Choosing two or three really descriptive adjectives can help to build up a picture for the reader. However, it can weaken your writing if you use unnecessary words, or **repeat** words that mean the same thing. For example:

> The priest was too intelligent, clever and wise to give a silly and stupid answer.

In this sentence, 'intelligent', 'clever' and 'wise' all mean the same thing, and so do 'silly' and 'stupid'.

A There are several ways of writing the following sentence in a shorter way that would mean the same thing. Rewrite the sentence below in two different, shorter ways without repeating the ideas.

The priest was too intelligent, clever and wise to give a silly and stupid answer.

B Write these sentences again in a briefer way, without changing their meanings.

1 *The pretty, attractive woman who went into the temple was holding a young baby, which she was carrying and the little tiny baby was crying and weeping loudly and noisily.*

2 *The great, huge, enormous congregation clapped and applauded when the choir of singers finished singing their happy, joyful new song.*

3 *The quiet church was silent, and I looked at the lovely, beautiful flowers, which smelled good and had a nice fragrance.*

Writing

Reports

A **report** is a piece of non-fiction writing that provides factual information. A report must:

- be organised into paragraphs
- be easy to follow
- give factual information.

To write a report you should:

- Research – use sources of information to find facts to include in your report. Remember to keep a list of the sources for your bibliography.
- Make notes – your notes should be short and in your own words, but you should copy out phrases and sentences that you want to quote in your report.
- Use your notes to write a first draft, then check it carefully and copy it neatly, adding a bibliography.

Here are some notes on Hinduism:

> main country where H. practised – India
> about 400 million Hindus in India
> main belief – reincarnation; what you come back as in the next life
> depends on how you lived this life
> 3 main gods – Brahma, Vishnu, Shiva
> Hindus worship in temples
> lots of celebrations
>
> Quote: 'Hinduism is a complex and varied religion, with many gods. Beliefs and practices vary from region to region.' (Mark Pearce in 'Hinduism')
>
> Books used:
> 'Hinduism' by Mark Pearce
> 'Life as a Hindu' by A. Sing
> 'World Religions' by Helen Dodd

Write a report about Hinduism, using:

- the notes above
- any relevant information from the report on pages 44–45
- your own knowledge of Hinduism
- any other facts you can discover by doing some research of your own.

The Night Sky

The planet Jupiter

At night you can see the stars twinkling in the vast expanse of outer space. There are billions of stars in the universe, and some of these may have planets like the Earth revolving around them. The universe seems to go on for ever, and no one knows exactly how many stars, planets and satellites it contains.

Our Solar System

The Sun lies at the centre of our solar system. It is vital to life on Earth. Without its heat and light, nothing could survive on our planet. In the larger world of the universe, however, the Sun is just one of millions and millions of quite ordinary stars. It is made of very light hydrogen gas. Nuclear reactions at its centre produce huge amounts of energy which leave the Sun as heat and light. The temperature at the centre of the Sun is an incredible 15 million degrees Celsius.

The Difference between Stars and Planets

Like the Sun, the other stars in the galaxy are glowing balls of gas held together by gravity. Reactions in the stars' centres produce heat and light. You can only see the planets and their moons because they reflect the Sun's light, but stars shine with their own light. They are all individual 'suns'.

The Vastness of the Universe

The stars are so far away that a special unit, called a 'light year', is used to measure the distances between them and the rest of the universe. A light year is the distance that light travels in a year – 9.5 million million kilometres.

A galaxy is an enormous group of stars. Our solar system lies in a galaxy called the Milky Way, which measures about 100,000 light years from side to side. (Compare this with the 8½ minutes which it takes for light to reach Earth from the Sun!) There are perhaps 100 thousand million stars in our galaxy, the Sun being only one, and there are thousands of millions of galaxies in the universe.

GLOSSARY

billion a thousand million (one billion = 1,000,000,000)

gravity a force that pulls things towards the Earth

million a thousand thousand (one million = 1,000,000)

planets objects which orbit (travel around) stars; the Earth is a planet

satellites objects in space which orbit planets

solar system a Sun and its system of stars, planets and moons, etc.

stars objects in space which give off light

universe all existing things – the Earth and all of space beyond it

Comprehension

A
1. What is essential to life on Earth?
2. How long does it take for the Sun's light to reach Earth?
3. Which is largest, our solar system, the universe or our galaxy?
4. What is the Milky Way and how big is it?
5. Is the Earth a star or a planet?

Day and night

The Earth spins around on its own axis once every 24 hours. The part of the Earth that is turned towards the Sun at any time experiences daylight. The part that is turned away from the Sun experiences night.

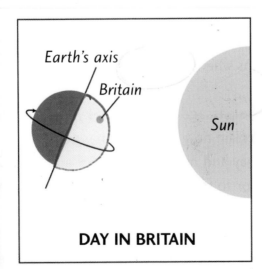

DAY IN BRITAIN

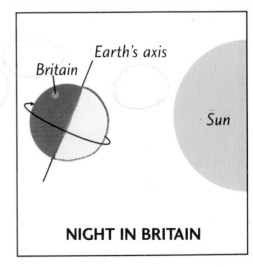

NIGHT IN BRITAIN

The planet Mars

The Seasons

The axis on which the Earth spins around the Sun is tilted. It is always tilted the same way and so we have different seasons depending on which part of the Earth is facing the Sun.

The Earth orbits (travels around) the Sun. During the Earth's orbit of the Sun, the part of the Earth that is tilted away from the Sun experiences winter. There are fewer hours of daylight, the Sun appears to be lower in the sky and it is colder. The part of the Earth that is tilted towards the Sun experiences summer. There are more hours of daylight, the Sun appears to be higher in the sky and it is warmer.

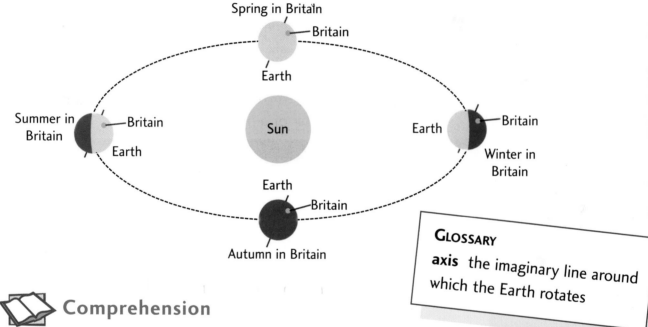

GLOSSARY

axis the imaginary line around which the Earth rotates

Comprehension

B 1 Explain in your own words why we have day and night.
2 Explain what happens when our part of the Earth is tilted away from the Sun.
3 Explain what happens when our part of the Earth is tilted towards the Sun.

C 1 Is the purpose of the passage 'The Night Sky', on page 52, to give information or to explain how something happens?
2 Is the purpose of 'Day and night' on page 53 and 'The Seasons' on page 54 to give information or to explain how something happens?
3 a How is the passage on page 52 illustrated?
   b How is 'Day and night', on page 53, illustrated?
   c Why do you think these types of illustrations have been used?

Vocabulary

Figures of speech

Remember, an **idiom** is a short phrase that usually means something quite different from what you might expect. For example:

> put your foot in it (means to say or do the wrong thing)

Similes and **metaphors** are ways of describing things by comparing them to other things. For example:

Simile: The stars gleamed <u>as</u> brightly as diamonds in a sky <u>like</u> black velvet.

Metaphor: The stars were diamonds in a black velvet sky.

Idioms, similes and metaphors are all called **figures of speech**. They are ways of describing feelings, thoughts or actions in a vivid way.

A Explain the meaning of each of these idioms.

1 he was over the moon   2 she has stars in her eyes
3 every cloud has a silver lining   4 the sky is the limit
5 it never rains but it pours   6 like water off a duck's back

Remember, **abstract nouns** are the names of qualities, feelings or times that you can't see, touch, taste, smell or hear. For example: bravery, happiness.

B 1 For each of the idioms below, find the abstract noun in the box that is closest to its meaning. Use a dictionary to check the meanings of any of the words in the box that are unfamiliar to you.

a having cold feet   b blowing one's own trumpet
c being under a cloud   d grasping the nettle
e throwing in the towel *defeatism*   f feathering one's own nest *selfishness*
g blowing hot and cold *indecision* h shedding crocodile tears *insincerity*

> *insincerity cowardice boastfulness ~~defeatism~~*
> *disgrace boldness ~~selfishness~~ ~~indecision~~*

2 Choose three of the idioms from question 1, and use each one in a sentence of your own.

Spelling

Pronouns and contractions

Possessive pronouns that describe nouns, for example, 'my telescope', can also be called **possessive adjectives**.

Some **pronouns** can be difficult to spell, either because they are part of a **contraction**, or because they sound similar to another pronoun. For example:

> they – a pronoun
>
> they're – a pronoun that is also a contraction, and means 'they are'
>
> theirs – a possessive pronoun that means 'belonging to them'

Remember, a **pronoun** stands in place of a noun. A **possessive pronoun** shows who owns something. A **contraction** is a word that is used in place of two words.

Here are some important sets of words that we use frequently.

Pronoun	Contraction	Possessive pronoun
it	it's (it is/it has)	its (belonging to it)
me		my (belonging to me)
		mine (belonging to me)
		our (belonging to us)
		ours (belonging to us)
you	you're (you are)	you (belonging to you)
	you've (you have)	yours (belonging to you)
	you'll (you will)	
they	they've (they have)	their (belonging to them)
	they'll (they will)	theirs (belonging to them)
	they're (they are)	

A Choose words from the box to fill the gaps in each sentence.

they'll	they're
their	there

1 _They'll_ be meeting later to go out with _their_ telescopes.

my	mine	me

2 I had _it_ for my birthday. Uncle Rob bought it for _me_ .

you	your	you're
you've	you'll	

3 If _you've_ looked at the stars before, _you_ have realised that _you'll_ need luck and a sharp eye if _you're_ to see a meteorite.

its	it's	it

4 _it_ is a pity _It's_ cloudy tonight, as the sky is not at _its_ best for watching the stars.

unit
Night **7**

56

B Write the contraction for each pair of words.

1 it is	2 he is	3 she is	4 we will
5 I will	6 she will	7 they will	8 we are
9 they are	10 you are	11 they have	12 you have

Grammar

Using 'has' and 'have'

There is a rule about when to use '**have**' and when to use '**has**'. 'Have' is used with most pronouns, except 'he', 'she', and 'it', when we use 'has'. For example:

They <u>have</u> been watching the stars.

She <u>has</u> been watching the stars.

A Copy and complete each sentence, using 'have' or 'has'.

1 "It _____ been a lovely evening," said Jessica.

2 "Yes, I _____ enjoyed it," said Kelly.

3 "The stars _____ been very bright," remarked Sam.

4 "That is because it _____ been so clear tonight," replied Uncle Colin.

5 "We _____ to leave now," said Kelly and Sam. "But we _____ had a great time."

6 "So _____ I," said Jessica. "It _____ been good fun."

B Write a sentence of your own, using each of the pronouns below and either 'have' or 'has'. The first one has been done to help you.

1 she

<u>She has finished her homework.</u>

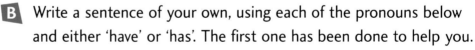

2 you   3 he   4 they   5 we

Punctuation

Practising direct speech

Remember that the comma goes inside the speech marks, not outside them!

A Copy these sentences, adding the speech marks and other missing punctuation.

1   That is a truly amazing sight said Mum

2   It certainly is replied Uncle Colin and it is incredible to think how far away some of the stars are

3   William added Just think the light from the stars has taken thousands of years to reach Earth

4   Is that true asked Jessica

5   It certainly is replied Uncle Colin though it's difficult to imagine

B Copy this paragraph, adding all the missing punctuation. Don't forget to begin a new line when a new person starts to speak.

Many of the stars are bigger than the Sun said Kelly Do they all have planets like our Earth asked Sam Yes replied Jessica but you can't see them from this distance So are there people like us on some of those planets asked Sam There could be said Jessica but no one can be sure Wouldn't it be funny if they were doing the same as us Maybe they are looking up and wondering if there could be people like them living on the planet called Earth laughed Kelly

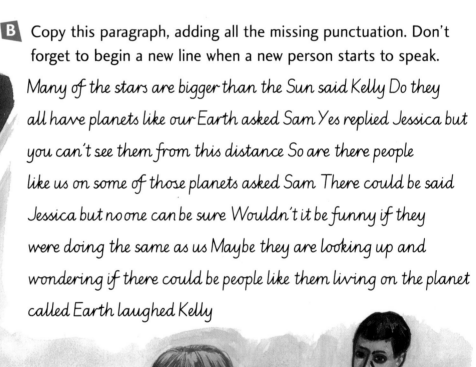

Writing

Explanations

'The Night Sky' is a piece of non-fiction writing that provides information. 'Day and Night' and 'The Seasons' are also non-fiction but their purpose is to **explain** how something happens. They use diagrams to help explain day and night and the seasons. Diagrams are very useful in non-fiction writing that explains something.

A Look at these two diagrams:

1. The diagram below shows an eclipse of the Moon (called a lunar eclipse). Study the diagram, then write an explanation of a lunar eclipse.

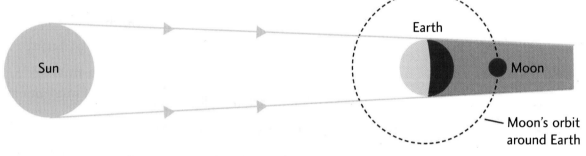

2. The diagram below shows an eclipse of the Sun (called a solar eclipse). Study the diagram, then write an explanation of a solar eclipse.

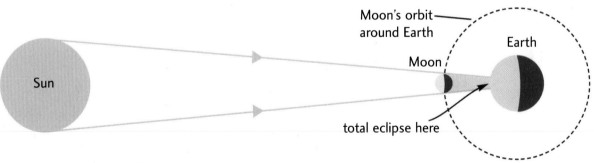

B Choose one of the following subjects.

- a seed growing into a flower
- how we breathe

Using text and diagrams, write an explanation of how your chosen subject happens. You may already know something about how it happens or you may have to do some research. When you do research, remember:

- make notes
- only copy from your sources if you are going to quote the exact words
- acknowledge your sources by writing a bibliography.

The Great Barrier Reef is a chain of 3,000 individual coral reefs off the coast of Australia, and is about 2,000 km long.

The word 'reef' comes from the old Viking word *rif*, which means 'rib' – an undersea danger to ships. When European sailors first arrived at shores surrounded by coral reefs, they were very aware that the sharp corals could tear the bottoms of their fragile boats. In time, the word rif became changed to 'reef'.

Coral reefs are made from limestone, formed from the skeletons of countless millions of tiny sea animals and plants. Each new generation fastens itself to the remains of previous generations' skeletons and, thus, coral reefs become massive structures.

Corals, and their companion plants, called algae, are some of the world's most incredible living things. These minuscule creatures manage to build reefs which can survive even hurricane-sized waves, a feat that many human-made structures cannot match. Corals also combine strength with beauty in their colourful branching shapes. Corals make the world's only living landscape.

Take care by reefs

It is fun to visit coral reefs while on holiday, but never venture to a coral reef without an adult and never go snorkelling without a qualified guide. The waves can be fierce and could throw you onto the sharp coral, while the currents can drag you out to sea. Remember, too, that the reef is a living organism, and some animals protect themselves by being poisonous.

How reefs form

Corals and algae are living things. They need special conditions to thrive, such as warm, clear water and light. Coral reefs develop when huge numbers of these creatures find just the right conditions to grow. Any rocky base, or even a rubbly mound, can be the home of reef-building coral, providing it is in warm, shallow, clear water.

Corals

Coral reefs are unique in nature's landscape because they are built by very simple animals and plants.

To know how reefs grow and change, it is very important to understand a little about the way corals live.

Coral skeletons

The skeleton of the coral is both an anchor when the polyp is waving about in the water, and a hiding place into which it can retreat when threatened. Because corals live in huge colonies, young corals build their skeleton homes on the old skeletons of their ancestors and, in this way, they can build a reef into a huge mass of limestone.

There are two basic types of coral – hard, or stony, corals and soft corals. Hard corals produce a limestone skeleton and are the reef-builders. Soft corals look much the same but they do not have a solid limestone skeleton, and only contain tiny limestone crystals within their tissues.

Be kind to corals

Reefs are easily damaged by collectors. Never collect samples from a reef.

What are corals?

Corals are composed of small animals called polyps, usually less than 3 mm in diameter, that belong to the same group of organisms as jellyfish and sea anemones. The polyps are housed in a limestone shell. Each polyp has a ring of tentacles which surrounds a central 'mouth'. The tentacles, which are fringed with tiny stinging hairs, catch tiny pieces of food, such as plankton, and push them into the mouth. The tentacles can withdraw into the limestone shell when necessary.

This type of coral is called 'brain coral'.

GLOSSARY

limestone a rock made up mainly of calcium carbonate
plankton the smallest forms of plant and animal in the sea
polyps the soft-bodied, anemone-like organisms of a coral
tentacles long, flexible feelers that can grip things

Comprehension

Don't forget the quote marks.

A Answer these questions by quoting the exact words from the text.
1 What are coral reefs made from?
2 What can corals and algae survive?
3 What are the two types of coral?
4 What conditions do coral reefs need to grow?

B Explain the following phrases in your own words.
1 human-made structures
2 coral reefs are unique
3 corals live in huge colonies
4 their ancestors

C For what purpose and for what audience do you think the passage was written?

Vocabulary

Onomatopoeia

Onomatopoeia is the word we use to describe words that sound similar to what they are describing. For example:

pop   splash   crackle

A 1 Sort the onomatopoeic words from the box into two lists, under the headings 'Sounds of the sea' and 'Sounds of the wind'.

> whistle   rustling   hum   shriek   rumble   drip
> thump   crash   roar   splashing

You might choose to put some words in both lists.

2 Add some words of your own to the lists you wrote in question 1.

B Think of some onomatopoeic words that describe the noise made by each of the following things. You could make up some words of your own.

1 a bonfire
2 a huge colony of birds
3 walking through thick mud
4 a baby

Spelling

Suffix 'ful'

Adding the **suffix 'ful'** to a word makes it into an adjective. For example:
hate + 'ful' = hateful
'hateful' means 'full of hate'

A 1 Add the suffix 'ful' to each word.

a *shame*　　b *faith*　　c *sorrow*　　d *deceit*

e *thought*　f *hope*　　g *fear*　　　h *wonder*

2 Use each word that you made in question 1 in a sentence of your own.

Remember, if a word ends with 'y', you usually need to change the 'y' to 'i' before adding a suffix. For example:
beauty + ful = beaut<u>i</u>ful

B 1 Use the suffix 'ful' to change each word into an adjective.

a *plenty*　　b *pity*　　c *mercy*　　d *fancy*

2 Make a list of as many words as you can that have the 'ful' suffix.

Grammar

Using pronouns

The words 'when' and 'where' are sometimes used as relative pronouns.

Remember, a **pronoun** takes the place of a noun. A **relative pronoun** is special because it does two jobs:

1 it takes the place of a noun

2 it acts as a conjunction, and is related to the noun that comes before it in a sentence.

For example:
　The nurse treated the girl. She had cut her foot on the coral.
　The nurse treated the girl <u>who</u> had cut her foot on the coral.

The relative pronoun 'who' relates to 'the girl' and acts as a conjunction to join the two sentences.

Relative pronouns are:
　who　　whom　　whose　　which　　that

'Who' is always used for people, 'which' and 'that' can be used for both people and things.

A Copy these sentences, using 'who' or 'that' to fill each gap.

1 The guide _____ took us to the reef said the currents were dangerous.

2 He told us about someone _____ had cut himself on the coral.

3 We went on a boat _____ had a glass bottom.

4 I wore the wetsuit _____ I had hired the day before.

You might need to change one or two words to make your new sentences.

B Rewrite each pair of sentences as a single sentence, using 'who', 'which' or 'whose' as a conjunction.

1 They said they had seen some sharks. The sharks had frightened them.

2 They told the guide. He said sharks were not usually dangerous.

3 The guide pointed to a shoal of beautiful fish. They were bright yellow.

4 I spoke to a tourist from Japan. He had never seen a coral reef before.

5 I helped the tourist. The tourist's camera had broken.

Sentence construction

Spoken and written language

Remember, a **sentence** needs at least one verb and one noun or pronoun. It must start with a capital letter and end with a full stop, a question mark or an exclamation mark.

A Copy these sentences, adding the punctuation and capital letters. Underline the verbs, nouns and pronouns in different colours.

1 we visited a reef on our last holiday

2 i saw the sharp, colourful coral from a glass-bottomed boat

3 are there sharks near the reef

4 the many types of coral we saw were incredibly beautiful

5 i dived down to the reef and it was an amazing experience

When you **speak**, you can use incomplete sentences, making yourself clear by using gestures and pauses, and showing your emotions in the way that you speak. When you **write**, you need to use properly punctuated, complete sentences so that somebody can read them at any time and know what they mean and what they are about.
For example, you might say:

"Out there. See?"

The meaning would be clear if you were speaking and pointing. However, if somebody read this, they would not know what you were writing about. A complete sentence that would be more helpful and informative would be:

Can you see the reef about two miles out to sea?

unit
Australia **8**

Remember, every sentence needs at least one verb.

B Look at the statements below. They might make sense to a listener, but they wouldn't be very clear to a reader. Write each one as a proper sentence that would make sense to a reader. Make sure you use correct punctuation.

1 They're really stunning.

2 See that there?

3 Don't get dragged out.

4 Look it's moving.

5 Hold this, OK.

6 Move those things.

Writing

Making notes

Remember, when you make **notes** you should:

- copy key words and phrases
- only copy the exact words if you want to use them as a quote
- keep a list of the sources from which you gather your information.

A
1 Carefully read pages 60–62 again.
2 Make notes on the information about coral reefs so you can write a **report** on what they look like. Find information about their:
   - colour
   - size
   - shape
   - location and the conditions they need to grow.
3 Use your notes, not the original passage, to write your report.

B
1 Carefully read pages 60–62 again.
2 Make notes on the parts of the passage that explain how coral reefs are formed.
3 Use your notes, not the original passage, to write an **explanation** of how coral reefs are formed.

Jamaica

Below is an extract from a travel brochure about holidays on the island of Jamaica

Jamaica is a tropical paradise, an island of colour and warmth lying in the shimmering blue waters of the Caribbean. The spectacular Blue Mountains are ringed with lush forests, magical plantations and incredible beaches. Palm trees sway in the warm breeze and luxurious hotels stand side by side with cosy, thatched self-catering apartments in welcoming resorts.

A holiday on the beautiful island of Jamaica offers something for everyone. If you enjoy an activity holiday, there are plenty of sports on offer, including paragliding, scuba diving, water-skiing and golf, to name but a few. If that is too energetic for you, then just relax in the warmth of the Caribbean sun and enjoy the beautiful surroundings.

Transport

The local taxis are reasonably cheap and are a good, safe way of getting about. Expect to pay about £15 for an 8 km journey.

Eating out

You will find no shortage of places to eat. Jamaica offers a range of excellent international cuisine, but do sample some of the delicious Caribbean food on offer, such as specialities like conch (a large shellfish).

Capital:	Kingston
Population:	2.4 million
Size:	6,790 square kilometres
Currency:	Jamaican $
Climate:	Average temperature 84° F Tropical thunderstorms in May & October
Health:	No vaccinations are necessary for tourists
Time difference:	5 hours behind Britain

Old Plantation House

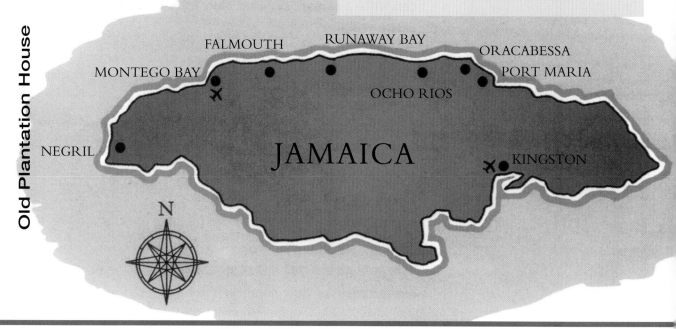

FALMOUTH   RUNAWAY BAY
MONTEGO BAY   ORACABESSA
                                   PORT MARIA
                  OCHO RIOS

NEGRIL   JAMAICA   KINGSTON

N

OCHO RIOS

One of Jamaica's top resorts is Ocho Rios. Its crescent-shaped, sandy beaches are lapped by clear, turquoise seas and backed by lush green mountains. It is ideally situated for visits to the Shaw Park Botanical Gardens and the spectacular Dunn's River Falls – a cool waterfall tumbling over a natural stone stairway. Ocho Rios is a small holiday town with a friendly, relaxed atmosphere, ideal for family holidays.

PALMS HOTEL			
	Prices in £ per person for 14 nights		
	Hotel room		
Number of people	4	3	2
1–19 May	629	659	729
20 May–2 June	649	679	749
3–23 June	659	689	759
24 June–7 July	689	719	789
8–21 July	699	739	809
22–28 July	769	799	869
29 July–18 August	799	829	899
19 August–1 September	759	789	859
2–15 September	699	729	799
16–29 September	679	699	779
30 Sept–20 October	659	679	759
21–31 October	669	689	769
1–8 November	599	639	699
9–24 November	579	619	679
25 Nov–4 December	569	599	659

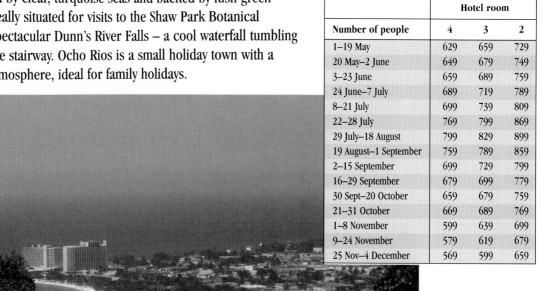

MONTEGO BAY

Montego Bay is Jamaica's second city and main tourist resort. It is a busy, lively place, ideal for those looking for a fun-packed, entertaining holiday. Attractions include rafting trips on the *Martha Brae* and the famous Doctor's Cave Beach.

MONTEGO GRAND HOTEL						
	Prices in £ per person for 14 nights					
	Hotel room			Self-catering apartment		
Number of people	4	3	2	4	3	2
1–19 May	639	669	759	649	699	799
20 May–2 June	659	689	789	669	719	829
3–23 June	659	689	789	679	729	839
24 June–7 July	689	739	829	719	779	879
8–21 July	699	749	839	729	789	889
22–28 July	749	779	899	789	829	959
29 July–18 August	779	829	929	819	879	989
19 August–1 September	749	779	889	779	819	939
2–15 September	699	749	839	729	789	889
16–29 September	679	729	819	709	769	863
30 Sept–20 October	659	689	789	679	729	839
21–31 October	659	689	789	679	729	839
1–8 November	629	659	749	649	689	799
9–24 November	599	639	729	629	669	769
25 Nov–4 December	579	619	699	599	649	749

 Comprehension

A 1 Where is Jamaica?
2 What sort of scenery would you expect to find in Jamaica?
3 What is the average temperature?
4 In which months are there likely to be tropical thunderstorms?
5 Which resort is situated near the Dunn's River Falls?

B Make a list of all the activities and places to visit that the travel brochure mentions.

C 1 The material in the travel brochure is presented in several different ways. Describe the various ways in which the information is presented and suggest reasons for using each type of presentation.
2 Write a paragraph to explain whether this travel brochure would persuade you to go to Jamaica on holiday. Give reasons for your answer.

Vocabulary

Using a thesaurus

A 1 Look up the following words in your thesaurus. Write down all the synonyms for each word.

    a   welcoming   b   relax   c   attractive

    d   rare   e   expensive   f   energetic

    2 Choose one synonym for each word from question 1 and use it in a sentence of your own about Jamaica.

B Use a thesaurus to help you make a list of as many words as possible that you might use to describe each of these features of Jamaica.

    1   the sea   2   the beaches   3   the mountains

    4   the food   5   the friendly people   6   the hotels

Spelling

Adding suffixes

Remember, the vowels are a, e, i, o and u.

> There are special rules for adding **suffixes** to words that end with an 'e'. If the suffix begins with a vowel, drop the 'e' before adding the suffix. For example:
>
>   live + 'ing' = living
>
> If the suffix begins with a consonant, keep the 'e'. For example:
>
>   live + 'ly' = lively

A 1 Add 'ing' to each word.

    a   *drive*   b   *criticise*   c   *revise*

    d   *make*   e   *breathe*   f   *practise*

    2 Add 'able' to each word.

    a   *cure*   b   *recognise*   c   *value*

    d   *believe*   e   *use*   f   *advise*

B 1 Add 'ly' to each word.

    a   *wise*   b   *nice*   c   *grave*

    d   *strange*   e   *brave*   f   *close*

    2 Add 'ful' to each word.

    a   *grace*   b   *hope*   c   *shame*

    d   *care*   e   *waste*   f   *use*

Grammar

Prepositions

Remember, **prepositions** tell us the position of something.

For example:

> Jamaica lies <u>in</u> the shimmering blue waters of the Caribbean.

Other prepositions include:

> beside   behind   through   around   among

Many prepositions are antonyms of other prepositions. For example:

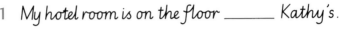

> near   far   above   below   in   out   under   over

A The prepositions have been omitted from these sentences. Write each sentence twice, using a different preposition each time.

1 My hotel room is on the floor _____ Kathy's.

2 The village was _____ the beach.

3 Yesterday, we drove _____ the town.

4 Today, I walked _____ the mountain.

5 The path went _____ the forest.

6 I could see a hut _____ the trees.

It doesn't matter if some of your sentences are a bit silly!

B Write a sentence of your own about Jamaica, using a preposition. Then see how many different meanings you can give the sentence by changing the preposition.

We often use **commas** between groups of two or more adjectives.
For example:

   It is a <u>busy, lively</u> place, ideal for those looking for a <u>fun-packed,
   entertaining</u> holiday.

A Copy these sentences, adding the missing commas.

1   Jamaica is a green hilly island.

2   I first saw Jamaica after a long tiring flight from Britain.

3   As I walked across the hot dusty airport runway, cold rainy
     England seemed a long way off.

4   The coach took me to my small comfortable apartment.

5   I had a relaxing enjoyable holiday in the sun.

B Copy and complete these sentences to add to the travel brochure
about Jamaica on pages 68–71. Add two adjectives to each
sentence and remember to include a comma between
the adjectives.

1   The _____ _____ seas around Jamaica are great for
     swimming.

2   Come and relax on the _____ _____ beaches.

3   Every day the sun shines from a _____ _____ sky.

4   When it is too hot, you can go and visit the _____
     _____ waterfalls.

5   Here, you can plunge in the _____ _____ pools.

Writing

Letters

Remember, to set out a **letter**, you need:

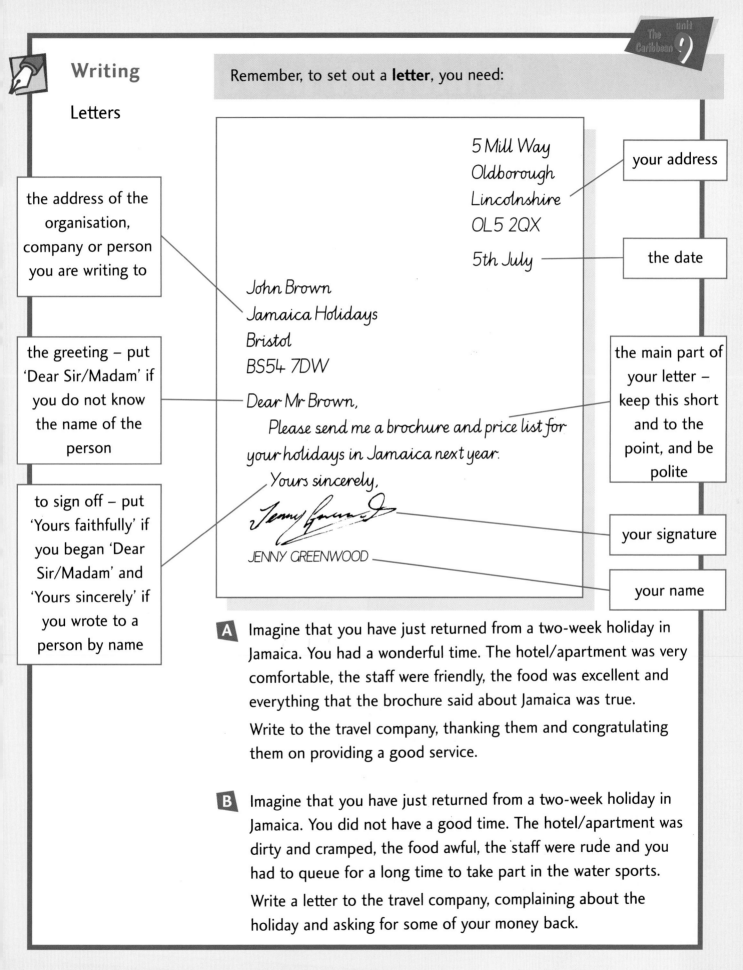

the address of the organisation, company or person you are writing to

the greeting – put 'Dear Sir/Madam' if you do not know the name of the person

to sign off – put 'Yours faithfully' if you began 'Dear Sir/Madam' and 'Yours sincerely' if you wrote to a person by name

5 Mill Way
Oldborough
Lincolnshire
OL5 2QX

5th July

John Brown
Jamaica Holidays
Bristol
BS54 7DW

Dear Mr Brown,

Please send me a brochure and price list for your holidays in Jamaica next year.

Yours sincerely,

Jenny Greenwood

JENNY GREENWOOD

your address

the date

the main part of your letter – keep this short and to the point, and be polite

your signature

your name

A Imagine that you have just returned from a two-week holiday in Jamaica. You had a wonderful time. The hotel/apartment was very comfortable, the staff were friendly, the food was excellent and everything that the brochure said about Jamaica was true.

Write to the travel company, thanking them and congratulating them on providing a good service.

B Imagine that you have just returned from a two-week holiday in Jamaica. You did not have a good time. The hotel/apartment was dirty and cramped, the food awful, the staff were rude and you had to queue for a long time to take part in the water sports.

Write a letter to the travel company, complaining about the holiday and asking for some of your money back.

Rainforests in Danger

The population of the world's rainforests is rising, but the rainforests themselves are shrinking!

During the twentieth century, huge areas of rainforest were cut down, while more and more people in countries like Brazil and Indonesia moved from crowded cities into rainforest areas in search of land. These people cleared areas of forest in order to build houses and grow crops. Unfortunately, once rainforest trees have been cut down and the undergrowth cleared, the soil is very easily washed away into the rivers by heavy rains. The soil that remains quickly loses its goodness and cannot produce crops. The farmers soon have to move on and clear new areas of land to farm.

As well as individual farmers, large companies also moved into the rainforests to exploit their rich resources. Vast stretches of forest have been felled by logging companies that export the valuable timber around the world. Mining companies have also destroyed enormous areas of rainforest by digging large mines. Cattle ranching to produce beef for countries like the USA has also meant that large areas of forest have been cut down to make room for the cattle.

The loss of so much of the world's rainforest is a serious problem. Scientists have warned that the destruction of the rainforests is harming the Earth and should be stopped. But why? The Earth's atmosphere is polluted with chemicals produced by industry and cars. Rainforest plants help to remove many of these dangerous gases from the atmosphere, as well as producing much of the oxygen that we breathe. Rainforests have been described as the lungs of the planet. They are essential to our survival. As well as

'Slash and burn' agriculture

keeping the air clean, scientists studying the plants believe that they can be used to produce many valuable medicines and may even provide the key to finding a cure for serious diseases, such as AIDS and cancer.

Some people from places like Europe and the USA claim that people should be prevented from using the rainforests. But using the forests is not wrong. People in rainforest areas depend on them as a source of income and food, and many have no other choice. In parts of Indonesia, the Government set up programmes to force poorer people to relocate from overcrowded areas into the rainforests.

So what is the solution? We just have to learn to use the rainforests' many resources in a way that will not destroy them forever. Governments can pass laws to protect their forests. Companies can create jobs elsewhere so that fewer people have to live and work in the rainforests. Timber companies can ensure that they plant new trees to replace those they cut down. New ways of farming in rainforests are being developed. In Brazil, for example, farmers are being encouraged to plant thin strips of land with crops, between which strips of

rainforest are left standing. This helps to prevent the soil from being washed away.

More than half the plants and animals that live in the world's rainforests do not exist anywhere else in the world. It is our responsibility to ensure that these forests are used wisely and are preserved for future generations.

Logging in a rainforest area

Comprehension

A Write whether each statement below is true or false.

F 1 The population of the world's rainforests is getting smaller.

F 2 Throughout the world the area covered by rainforests is gradually increasing.

T 3 Rainforest is sometimes cleared so that local people can grow crops, or for mining to take place.

F 4 Rainforest trees use up oxygen from the air.

T 5 When areas of rainforest are cleared, soil is more easily washed away by heavy rain.

B Make notes on the things you would say in these situations:

1 Imagine you are a farmer in a rainforest area. You are visited by people who try to persuade you not to chop down any more trees in the rainforest. What would you say to them?

2 What could people from Britain do to help stop the destruction of the rainforests?

C How persuasive do you find the passage?
Does it persuade you that:
- the rainforests should be protected?
- the local people have the right to use the land?
- people from other countries have the right to use the timber and clear the ground for mining?
Give reasons for your answers.

Vocabulary

Using a dictionary

Dictionaries contain lots of information about each word:
- its definition
- what word class (part of speech) it is
- its origin, in some cases
- related words or sayings, if any.

---

junk (1) *n* valueless rubbish.

junk (2) *n* a Chinese sailing ship.

jurisdiction *n* authority, legal power.

juror *n* a member of a jury.

jury *n* a group of twelve persons who decide in a court of law whether an accused person is guilty or not (*pl.* **juries**).

just (1) *adj* fair, right, as *a just decision*.

just (2) *adv* 1. barely, as *he has just left*. 2. exactly, as *the money is just right*.

    just now at present.

    just then a moment ago.

justice *n* fairness.

    to do justice to oneself to do one's best.

Justice of the Peace (in England) a magistrate who tries small offences.

justify *v* to defend, to say why something that has been done was right; as *Tom justified his absence from the meeting* (**justifying, justified**), *adj.* **justifiable** shown to be right; **justification** defence, as *there is no justification for what you have done*.

jut *v* to stick out (**jutting, jutted**).

juvenile *adj* 1. young. 2. suitable for young people, as *juvenile books*. **juvenile** *n.* a young person.

A Look at the dictionary extract above.

1 Write the correct spelling of each word below.

    a *juresdiction*   b *justise*   c *juvinile*

2 Which word follows 'jut'?

3 What word class is 'jury'?

4 What is a 'juror'?

5 What does 'to do justice to oneself' mean?

6 What are the two quite different meanings of 'junk'?

7 Which word can be both an adjective and a noun?

The words in a dictionary are in alphabetical order but, to make it easier to find a word, there are **guide words** at the top of each page. These tell you the first word and the last word that appear on that page. To find a word, you need to find the page on which your word comes <u>after</u> the first guide word and <u>before</u> the second one.
For example, if the guide words on a page are JOVIAL and KEEP, the first word on the page is 'jovial' and the last word on the page is 'keep'. The word 'jug' would be on this page.

B Here are the guide words from three different pages in a dictionary:

Page 128:   lorry   lunar
Page 129:   lunatic   mail
Page 177:   radical   ranger

Write the number of the page on which each of the following words would appear.

1	maggot	2	lynch	3	raffle	4	rally
5	loud	6	lowland	7	ludicrous	8	lunacy
9	range	10	lyric	11	radical	12	lorry

Spelling

Antonyms

Many **antonyms** are made by adding **prefixes** to root words.
For example:

    well   <u>un</u>well   possible   <u>im</u>possible   legal   <u>il</u>legal

Here is a table of some common prefixes that can make antonyms.

Prefix	Meaning	Example
anti √	against	anticlockwise
dis √	away, off	dismount
ex √	out of	export
im √	into	import
in √	not	incapable
il	not	illegal
ir √	not	irresponsible
mis √	wrong	misbehave
non √	not	nonsense
un √	not	untidy

A Copy each sentence below, using a prefix to make the sentence mean the opposite. The first one has been done to help you.

1   The jigsaw is complete.

The jigsaw is incomplete.

2   I feel certain about what I should do.

3   You were very polite to Tina.

4   I agree with you.

5   I approve of what you are doing.

B Look at the table of prefixes in the box on page 80. Write down at least two other examples of words using each prefix. Use your dictionary to help you.

Grammar

Writing for your audience

Remember, when you are writing, it is important to think carefully about who will be reading what you write. You should write in a way that suits your **audience**. You might write in a relaxed style for family and friends, and in a formal style if you are giving information or writing a letter to someone you don't know.

A Imagine that you are a farmer in a rainforest area. You have decided to write a letter to a British politician, explaining why you need to clear areas of rainforest. Your letter should be in a formal style. Write just a few sentences that might go into the letter.

B Look at your answer to part A. Now write a few sentences that you might put into a letter to a close friend, or a relative who lives a long way away, explaining why you must clear areas of forest.

Sentence construction

Clauses

Remember, a **clause** is part of a sentence that contains a verb.

A **main clause** contains at least one verb and makes sense on its own. A **subordinate clause** helps the main clause but does not make sense on its own. For example:

The soil gets washed away <u>when heavy rain falls.</u>

| main clause | subordinate clause |

'The soil gets washed away' makes sense by itself, so it is a main clause. 'when heavy rain falls' does not make sense on its own and is a subordinate clause.

Subordinate clauses are often joined to main clauses by conjunctions or pronouns, such as:

Conjunctions:							
although	before	so	until	unless	as	because	if

Pronouns:				
who	whose	which	that	when

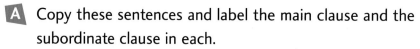

A Copy these sentences and label the main clause and the subordinate clause in each.

1 *Life can be hard for people who live in rainforest areas.*

✓ 2 *Farming should be planned carefully so rainforests aren't destroyed.*

3 *It is important that we solve this problem before all the rainforests are destroyed.*

B To each main clause below, add a subordinate clause of your own that begins with the word in brackets.

1 *The world's rainforests contain a variety of birds and animals (that)*

2 *Many rainforest dwellers are very poor people (who)*

3 *Scientists are seeking new ways to farm (so)*

Writing

Writing to persuade

Information can be presented in different ways. The passage on pages 76–77 is quite long and needs careful reading. The same sort of information could be presented as a **leaflet**, with simple drawings and captions to make it easier for a younger person to read. It would also be more eye-catching and might be more persuasive.

You are going to plan and make a leaflet to persuade people that the rainforests must be protected.

Fold

Stage 1
Fold an A4 piece of paper in half.

Stage 2
On the front of the leaflet, you need a drawing of a rainforest and an eye-catching title that will let the reader know what the leaflet is about.

Stage 3
Read again the passage on pages 76–77. Make notes about how and why rainforests are being destroyed. Open your leaflet and, on the left-hand side, draw and caption small pictures to show how and why the rainforests are being destroyed.

Stage 4
Using the passage on pages 76–77, make notes about why rainforests should not be destroyed. On the right-hand side of your leaflet, draw and caption small pictures to show why the rainforests should not be destroyed.

The Loch Ness Monster

Every year, thousands of tourists from around the world visit Loch Ness in Scotland in the hope of seeing the prehistoric creature, affectionately known as 'Nessie', that is said to inhabit the murky waters of the loch.

The earliest stories about the monster go back to AD 565 when the Irish saint, Columba, is said to have seen it. One story says that a disciple of Columba was swimming across the loch when the monster appeared suddenly 'with a great roar and open mouth'. Saint Columba made the sign of the cross, asked for God's protection and said to it, 'Think not to go further, nor touch not that man. Quick, go back.' The monster is said to have obeyed and nobody has ever claimed to have been hurt by Nessie.

Divers prepare to set up an underwater camera in the hope of photographing the monster.

Over the last fourteen centuries there have been many recorded sightings of Nessie, but it wasn't until 1934 that the monster was allegedly captured in a photograph. Robert Kenneth Wilson, a London surgeon holidaying in Scotland, was driving past the loch and took a photograph of what he claimed was the monster. It showed a long neck and a thick body and was published in the *London Daily Mail*.

Opinion was divided over the photograph. Those who really believed that the monster existed said that the photograph fitted the description given by others who claimed to have seen it. Those who did not believe in the monster said that the photograph showed rotting vegetation floating on the surface, or perhaps the tail of a diving otter.

One day in 1951, Lachlan Stuart, a forestry worker living by the loch, went out to milk his cows at 6.30 a.m. He noticed that the surface of the water was disturbed and three humps appeared and moved in a line towards the shore. He went quickly back to his house, grabbed his camera and managed to take one photograph before the shutter jammed and whatever it was disappeared beneath the waters of the loch. This photograph was argued over in the same way that Mr Wilson's had been seventeen years before.

The first moving pictures of what might be Nessie were taken in 1960. Tim Dinsdale was so convinced by what he had seen and photographed that he gave up his job and lived in a small boat on the loch, spending all his time in search of the monster. His enthusiasm and determination made others take the whole subject more seriously and the first of many scientific investigations began.

In 1961, the Loch Ness Phenomena Investigations Bureau was formed by two naturalists and a man called David James, who was a Member of Parliament. James recorded all the known sightings of the monster and set up 24 cameras all around the loch to try to photograph the elusive creature. Unfortunately, the cameras failed to get any shots and, to this day, there is no conclusive proof that the Loch Ness monster really exists.

The photograph taken in 1934 by Robert Wilson

Loch Ness, Scotland

Comprehension

A
1. When was the monster first photographed?
2. What did people think of the photograph?
3. Who claimed to have photographed the monster in 1951?
4. Who gave up his job to search for the monster?

B Find the following words and phrases in the passage and write in your own words what you think each one means.

1. murky waters
2. disciple
3. allegedly
4. opinion was divided
5. elusive
6. conclusive

C Carefully read the passage again.

1. Make notes on any relevant information that supports the belief that the monster exists.
2. Make notes on any relevant information that does not support the belief that the monster exists.

Strange Stories unit 11

86

Vocabulary

'ist' letter pattern

The '**ist**' letter pattern often comes at the end of a word. Many 'ist' words are nouns that are the names of people who have specific interests. For example:

a <u>naturalist</u> studies natural things – animals and plants

A Use a dictionary to help you find out what these people study.

1 biologist   2 geologist   3 zoologist

4 botanist   5 chemist   6 climatologist

B Use each of these nouns in a sentence of your own to show that you know what it means. Use your dictionary to help you.

1 pharmacist   2 pacifist   3 ornithologist

4 reflexologist   5 physicist   6 graphologist

7 meteorologist   8 terrorist   9 florist

Spelling

Suffixes

Remember, **abstract nouns** are the names of things we can't see or touch, such as qualities, feelings and emotions.

Verbs can often be made into nouns by adding a **suffix**. For example:

Verb: You <u>amaze</u> me.

Noun: She looked at him in <u>amaze**ment**</u>.

A Make an abstract noun from each verb below by addng a suffix from the box. You may need to change some words slightly when you add the suffix. Use a dictionary to check your spelling.

ment	ure	ion	ation

1 agree   2 depart   3 express

4 fix   5 enjoy   6 involve

7 relax   8 fail   9 pollute

10 replace   11 improve   12 please

B Write the verb from which each of these abstract nouns was made, and the suffix that was added.

1 entertainment   2 compensation   3 pressure

4 consideration   5 detachment   6 excitement

87

Grammar

'I' and 'me'

It can be difficult to know when to use 'I' and when to use 'me'.

For example:

> Which is correct, 'My brother and I went shopping.' or 'My brother and me went shopping.'?

To check, imagine taking away the words before 'I' or 'me'. For example:

> (My brother and) me went shopping.

This sounds wrong!

> (My brother and) I went shopping.

This sounds right! 'My brother and I went shopping.' is correct.

A Copy these sentences, using either 'I' or 'me' in each gap.

1 Suzy invited Vikram and _____ to her party.

2 She asked if Vikram and _____ would bring some games.

3 She also asked Vikram and _____ to bring some paper cups.

4 Vikram and _____ missed the bus so we were late.

5 Suzy told Vikram and _____ to put on some music.

6 Vikram and _____ danced to our favourite music.

B Rewrite each pair of sentences as a single sentence. The first one has been done to help you. You may need to change some words.

1 Jake is going to Suzy's party. I am going to Suzy's party.

   Jake and I are going to Suzy's party.

2 Laura is dancing with Ross. Laura is dancing with me.

3 Hamish is cross with Ross. Hamish is cross with me.

4 Julia saw a rare bird. I saw a rare bird.

5 Leo is going to help Patsy. Leo is going to help me.

6 Tom has had his tonsils out. I have had my tonsils out.

Punctuation

Apostrophes for contractions

Remember, a **contraction** is a way of making a word shorter or joining two words to make one word. We put an **apostrophe** in place of the letter or letters that have been left out. Contractions are usually made from words that we run together when we speak. For example:

<u>wasn't</u> is a contraction of 'was not'

A Write the contraction for each of these.

1 there is   2 cannot   3 it will

4 we shall   5 must not   6 they have

7 would not   8 you are   9 has not

B Copy these sentences, replacing each pair of coloured words with a contraction.

1 "I am sure there is a monster," said James.

2 "You will need proof if I am to believe you," I replied.

3 "I have taken some photos," he said.

4 "Well, I have not seen anything yet," I said.

5 "I do not think you are keeping an open mind," he complained grumpily.

Writing

Constructing an argument

Putting forward an **argument** in writing needs very careful thought. You may be writing to support one side of an argument, or you may be presenting both sides and allowing your reader to make up his or her own mind. These are the stages:

- Stage 1 – research
- Stage 2 – making notes
- Stage 3 – ordering your notes
- Stage 4 – writing a first draft
- Stage 5 – checking the first draft
- Stage 6 – writing the final copy.

Stage 3 is probably the most difficult. Once you have looked at lots of reference books and made your notes, you have to sort them into order so that your reader can easily follow what you write. The way to do this is to plan what each paragraph is going to be about.

A Look again at the passage on pages 84–85. There are seven paragraphs and each one tells you something different about the Loch Ness Monster.

Copy and complete the table below.

Paragraph	What it is about
1	Introduces the Loch Ness monster so the reader knows what the passage is going to be about.

B This is the picture taken by Lachlan Stuart in 1951:

Imagine you are a naturalist who has been asked to study the photograph and report what you think. You have not yet formed an opinion as to whether or not the monster exists.

Make notes and write your report in four paragraphs:

Paragraph 1

Describe in detail what you see in the picture.

Paragraph 2

Give all the reasons you can for this being a photograph of the Loch Ness monster.

Paragraph 3

Give all the reasons you can for this not being a photograph of the Loch Ness monster.

Paragraph 4

Come to a conclusion, giving your opinion after studying the photograph and weighing the evidence.

Advertising

Advertisements surround us in our daily lives – on the television, on posters, in newspapers and magazines, on the Internet. Everywhere, we are faced with words and pictures trying to persuade us that we really need to buy certain things to improve our lives. Opposite is an advertisement for a theme park.

 Comprehension

A Look at the poster on the opposite page.
1 What is the poster advertising?
2 Who is the advertisement aimed at?
3 Make a list of the words and phrases in the advertisement that are used to persuade you to visit Dragon World.
4 Why do you think the advertiser has used a little rhyme in the advert?

B Explain whether or not the advert would make you want to visit Dragon World. Give your reasons.

Dragon World

Spend a Day with Dragons

A fantastic day out for all the family
It's the dragon experience you'll never forget!

Special introductory offer:
Family ticket half price

Access to all the rides for two adults and up to four children

Just off the M47 at junction 23

Dragon World
junction 23
M47

Featuring the biggest, scariest dragon ride in the world!

Come inside the dragons' lair
You'll never have a scarier scare!

Vocabulary

Abbreviations and acronyms

When we speak, we often use shortened forms of words. These are called **abbreviations**. Sometimes, the original word or words gradually go out of use until we only use the shortened version. For example:

At 11 o'(f the) clock, I (tele)phoned to say my (omni)bus had been cancelled.

Some names are abbreviated. For example:

Will(iam)   Matt(hew)   (E)Liz(abeth)

A Write the abbreviation we use for each name or word.

1 influenza   2 Patricia

3 perambulator   4 electronic mail

5 aeroplane   6 petroleum

7 All Hallows evening 8 Frederick

9 photograph   10 facsimile

Some groups of words, especially the names of organisations, can be shortened by using just the first letter or few letters of each of the main words. This is called an **acronym**. For example:

NSPCC is an acronym for 'National Society for the Prevention of Cruelty to Children'

Sometimes, the letters in an acronym make another word. Instead of saying all the letters, we pronounce the acronym as a word. For example:

OXFAM is an acronym for the 'OXford Committee for FAMine Relief'

Some of them are acronyms for more than one thing!

B Use your dictionary and reference books to discover what these acronyms stand for.

1 RSPCA   2 p.m.   3 EU   4 UNESCO
5 RAF   6 ETA   7 NATO   8 www
9 p.s.   10 CD-ROM   11 PC   12 BASIC

Spelling

'ent' and 'ant'
word endings

Many adjectives end with 'ent' or 'ant'. For example:

silent   ignorant

These words can be made into abstract nouns by changing 'ent'
endings to 'ence', and 'ant' endings to 'ance'. For example:

silence   ignorance

A Copy and complete this table.

Adjectives	Nouns
distant	
	obedience
tolerant	
	violence
intelligent	
	importance
evident	
	independence
absent	
	abundance
innocent	
	arrogance
resistant	

B 1 Choose two nouns from part A and use them in sentences of
       your own.
   2 Choose two adjectives from part A and use them in sentences
       of your own.
   3 Choose two adjectives from part A that can be made into
       adverbs by adding 'ly'. Make them into adverbs and use them
       in sentences of your own.

95

Grammar

did/done and
doesn't/don't

Never use an auxiliary verb with '**did**.' Always use an auxiliary verb with '**done**'. For example:

The boys <u>did</u> their best not to get too excited.

The boys <u>had</u> <u>done</u> their best not to get too excited.

A Copy these sentences, using the correct verb.

1 The workers had <u>did/done</u> well to get Dragon World ready in time.

2 They <u>did/done</u> extra work every day for several weeks.

3 "They couldn't have <u>did/done</u> more," said the manager.

4 Simon <u>did/done</u> more hours than anyone.

5 "He has <u>did/done</u> an excellent job," said the manager.

6 The police <u>did/done</u> their best to keep the traffic moving.

Doesn't is the contraction for 'does not'. We use it with singular nouns and the singular pronouns 'he', 'she' and 'it'. For example:

Raj <u>doesn't</u> want to go home yet.
He <u>doesn't</u> want to go home yet.

Don't is the contraction for 'do not'. We use it with plural nouns and the pronouns 'I', 'you', 'we' and 'they'. For example:

The children <u>don't</u> want to go home yet.
They <u>don't</u> want to go home yet.

B 1 Use the correct contraction to complete each sentence.

a "I <u>doesn't/don't</u> want to go home!" cried Libby.

b "We <u>doesn't/don't</u> either," agreed Holly and Emma.
"You <u>doesn't/don't</u> have a choice," said Mr Brown.

c "The theme park <u>doesn't/don't</u> stay open after six o'clock!"

d "Jake <u>doesn't/don't</u> feel very well," said Emma.

e "Make sure he <u>doesn't/don't</u> eat any more candy floss," begged Mr Brown. "It <u>doesn't/don't</u> agree with him!"

2 Write two sentences of your own to finish the conversation in question 1, using 'don't' in one and 'doesn't' in the other.

Punctuation

Apostrophes for possession

Remember, to make a <u>singular</u> noun into a **possessive noun**, we add an apostrophe and then an 's'. For example:

The girl<u>'s</u> camera was broken.

Singular noun: girl   Possessive noun: girl<u>'s</u>

To make most <u>plural</u> nouns into possessive nouns, we just add an apostrophe. For example:

The two girls<u>'</u> cameras were broken.

Plural noun: girls   Possessive noun: girls<u>'</u>

But, when plural nouns do not end with an 's', we add an apostrophe and then an 's' (in the same way as making a singular noun into a possessive noun). For example:

The four men<u>'s</u> coats.

Plural noun: men   Possessive noun: men<u>'s</u>

A Rewrite these phrases using possessive nouns. The first one has been done to help you.

1 the feathers belonging to the birds   *the birds' feathers*

2 the ball belonging to the boy

3 the calves belonging to the cow

4 the costumes belonging to the actors

5 the sandwiches belonging to the children

6 the beards belonging to the men

7 the cars belonging to the women

B Copy these phrases, adding the missing apostrophes.

1 the two girls biscuits

2 the three womens jobs

3 this schools uniform is blue

4 the two boys game

5 the three teachers tea

6 that boys bag

Writing

Advertisements

Let's look at how **advertisements** work. People who write advertisements are trying to persuade you to buy their product. They make an advertisement attractive and eye-catching so you will notice it. They think carefully about what an advertisement looks like and who it is aimed at. They consider the following points.

- Colour – They usually use bright colours. They may use colours that clash to make the advert more striking. They may use black and white, which is eye-catching.
- Layout – This has to be clear and easy to read, but may look quite 'busy' if there is lots of information to read. The name of what is being advertised must stand out.
- Illustrations – They may use drawings, photographs or diagrams, or all three. Most advertisements have some sort of illustration.

The words advertisers use are very important. They may use:

- Persuasive language – The advertiser tries to make you feel that you really need this product. The advert will usually try to persuade you that you really need their product and that it is the best one on the market.
- Slogans – These can be catchy and may rhyme. They stick in your mind so you remember the product.
- Information – Advertisements usually contain information about what the product can do for you, as well as giving you the price and details of where you can buy it.

Design your own advertisement in the form of a leaflet or poster for one of the following:

- a Tudor house where you can see the actual furniture, cooking utensils, etc. that were used during the reign of Henry VIII
- a new water theme park, with swimming pools, water slides, a wave machine, etc.
- a new magazine about a sport or hobby
- a new type of fizzy drink.

First, think of an interesting name for your place/product. Then, plan your advertisement and make notes before you begin. You need to think about:

- who your advertisement is aimed at
- how you will make it eye-catching
- what language you will use to persuade people to visit/buy what you are advertising.

Check-up

 Vocabulary

A Copy each word and write its **root word**, then write down as many other words as possible from the same **word family**. Use a dictionary to help you.

1 *completion*   2 *approval*   3 *caring*   4 *complicated*

B Using your thesaurus, write down as many **synonyms** as possible for each word below. Then, write the synonyms of each word in order, from 'least' to 'most'.

1 small   2 happy   3 slow   4 large

C Make an **adverb** from each word below.

1 *guilt*   2 *easy*   3 *clever*   4 *angry*

5 *quiet*   6 *busy*   7 *careful*   8 *gentle*

D Write whether each word has an **antonym** and, if so, what it is.

1 many   2 curved   3 dog   4 correct

5 house   6 polite   7 capable   8 honest

E Write in your own words the meaning of each of the following **figures of speech**.

1 let off steam   2 see the light

3 put your foot in it   4 keep your hair on

F Use your dictionary to find out and write down:

- the **word class**
- the **definition**
- the **origin**

of each word below.

1 orator   2 sociable   3 tunic   4 wince

G What would you call a person who studies

1 geology?   2 science?   3 physics?   4 chemistry?

Spelling

A Write the **plural** of each of each noun.

1 tomato   2 cockatoo   3 planet   4 valley

5 difficulty   6 torch   7 knife   8 cliff

B Copy all the words from the box that have a **soft 'c'**.

| celebrate | catch | face | ice | accident | can | carry | century |

C Sort the words from the box into two lists: **possessive pronouns** and **contractions**.

| his | they've | yours | they'll | I'm | hers | theirs | you're |
| ours | it's | you'll | mine | you've | its | they're |

D Add the **suffix** to each word.

1 achieve + 'able'   2 surprise + 'ing'   3 mercy + 'ful'   4 free + 'ly'

5 thought + 'ful'   6 safe + 'ly'   7 fancy + 'ful'   8 receive + 'ing'

E Make an **abstract noun** from each verb below, by adding a **suffix** from the box.

| ment | ure | ion | dom |

1 confine   2 discuss   3 free   4 press

5 amaze   6 confess   7 depart   8 operate

F 1 Add **'ant'** or **'ent'** to complete each adjective.

a assist_____   b depend_____   c insol_____   d petul_____

2 Write the abstract noun that can be made from each of your answers to question 1.

Grammar

A Copy these sentences, filling each gap with **'anything'** or **'nothing'**.

1 They couldn't find in the cupboard _____ to eat.

2 There was _____ they could do to stop him.

3 We wouldn't do _____ until Joel arrived.

B Copy each sentences twice, putting the speaker's name in a different place each time.

1 "I know you want a new computer game, but I simply can't afford it," said Mum.

2 "Yes, I will get you one for your birthday," said Mum.

C 1 Rewrite this sentence as **reported speech**.

"Are you coming to see our concert, Nan?" asked Jessica.

2 Rewrite this sentence as **direct speech**.

Jessica's Nan told her that she was very much looking forward to the concert.

D Copy and complete these past-tense sentences by adding '**was**', '**were**', '**have**' or '**has**'.

1 We _____ looking forward to our holiday.

2 I _____ really excited about it.

3 My parents _____ booked a cottage for a week.

4 Mum _____ bought a map.

E Write the words from the box in four lists: **common nouns, proper nouns, collective nouns** and **abstract nouns**.

sadness	troop	bath	Brian	comic	herd	misery	book	London
fright	Tuesday	squad	temple	Muslims	anger	team	water	crowd

F Write a sentence about your classroom which includes a **preposition**. Then, write the sentence as many times as you can, changing the preposition each time.

G Copy these sentences, using '**who**' or '**that**' to fill each gap.

1 This is the picture _____ I painted.

2 I hugged the boy, _____ was my friend.

3 I ate an apple _____ was unripe.

H Copy these sentences, using '**I**' or '**me**' to fill each gap.

1 Danny and _____ had tea.

2 Mum gave Sue and _____ some sweets.

3 Lou helped Kim and _____.

4 Tim and _____ were late.

I 1 Write whether '**doesn't**' or '**don't**' goes with each pronoun.

    a I   b she   c they   d you   e we

  2 Write whether '**did**' or '**done**' completes each phrase.

    a I _____ it b he has _____ it c they _____ it d we have _____ it

Punctuation and sentence construction

A Copy and complete this table.

Verb family	Past tense (1)	Past tense (2)	Past tense (3)
to shout	he shouted	he was shouting	he had shouted
to hide	she _____	she _____ _____	she _____ _____
to run	I _____	I _____ _____	I _____ _____
to think	we _____	we _____ _____	we _____ _____
to teach	you _____	you _____ _____	you _____ _____

B 1 Change these sentences from **active** to **passive**.

    a The girl threw crumbs to the birds.

    b James ate a huge meal.

  2 Change these sentences from **passive** to **active**.

    a We were shown to our seats by the stewardess.

    b Gail was given a new bike by her dad.

C Copy these sentences, adding the **speech marks** and other **punctuation**.

  1 Can you come to my house tonight asked Julie

  2 Yes said Ann but I mustnt be late getting home

  3 We can do our homework and then watch that programme on TV said Julie and then we will have something to eat

D Copy these sentences, adding two **adjectives** and the missing **comma** to each one.

  1 The _____ _____ house stood on the hill.

  2 The _____ _____ boat bobbed on the lake.

E Join each pair of sentences with a **conjunction**, to make a **compound sentence**.

1 I ran all the way. I was late.   2 He broke his pen. I lent him mine.

F Copy these sentences and use different colours to underline the **main** and **subordinate clauses** in each one.

1 James is my friend and always will be.

2 I'm enjoying the book that I bought yesterday.

G Copy and complete each sentence, adding the missing **apostrophes**.

1 The two boys jackets havent been found.

2 The boys bag wouldnt fit in his locker.

3 Youll tread on the dogs tail if youre not careful.

4 Im preparing our three dogs dinners.

Writing

Read the starting point very carefully. Choose one of the writing tasks to do.

Write a front-page newspaper report based on the starting point. Remember to include an eye-catching headline, facts and opinions.

Write a first-person account, as though you had witnessed a strange but true event.

Think about who could be involved in a factual event that might be written about under the title 'Strange but true'. Interview this person. Think carefully about the questions you want to ask, the likely responses and the way you will set out the written interview.

Make notes on an unusual happening that could be described as 'strange but true'. In the third person, write a clear explanation of what occurred and how it occurred.

Story starting point: Strange but true

Think of a real event that could be described as 'strange but true'. Write a report about the event, designed to persuade people that it really did happen.

Choose an unusual event that could be described as 'strange but true' and write a balanced report about it, looking at all the evidence that might prove it was true and all the evidence that might prove it was untrue.